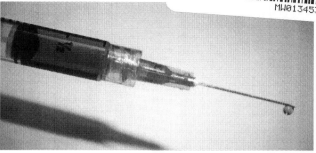

Returning to

the Light

✞

Paul Williamson

Copyright © 2016 Paul Williamson
All rights reserved.

ISBN: 1530920876
ISBN 13: 9781530920877

Contents

Introduction	Page **5**
The Journey	Page **7**
Prayer Strategies	Page **67**
Practical Helps	Page **81**
Epilogue	Page **105**
Patrick's Words	Page **121**
Conclusion	Page **125**

Introduction

My wife, Anne, and I were married in our late teens. We are the parents of eleven children and the grandparents of nineteen. We live in a small Pennsylvania community and have never lived more than five miles from our birthplace.

Lifelong Catholics, we have been involved in youth ministry and adult religious education since 1977. Having a large family together has been our mutual desire since we experienced a reciprocal love at first sight in high school. Our son Patrick, on whom this writing is centered, claims the title of our middle child.

Though we don't have degrees in psychology or counseling, we have learned much in both of these fields. This education has been garnered while raising our family. The school of life has been our tutor. And a faith in God has been our guide.

The purpose of this writing is to help other families. For those not currently influenced by drug addiction, I hope that these words can aid in preventing such an occurrence. For those who are experiencing problems with drug addiction, I hope that through our experience, they will find a way out of this confounding and tragic nightmare.

This is also written for the addict. I hope that you will find in this writing the utter futility and the ultimate agony that addiction carries upon its back. And I hope that through my son's experience, the drug abuser sees that there is a way out.

Above all, I want to promote the theological virtue of hope—for without hope, the battle is already lost. I've learned that no person is beyond redemption. There is nobody who cannot be saved. I've learned that no one is hopeless. If there is just one thing that you will take away from this reading, let it be that you should never, ever give up hope on anyone.

Humans, made in the image and likeness of God, have the ability to rise above their current situation and become new people. The lowest of the low can one day be among the most esteemed. This path is not easy, but it is possible.

Walk with me as I take you along the path leading into addiction. Ache with me as I take you along the path of active drug use. Pray with me as I look for the right path to follow. Rejoice with me as I skip along the path to recovery. Come along with me as I travel from darkness to light. Watch with me as my son embarks on the path of returning to the light.

The Journey

Patrick and his friend were at a party. Drugs were everywhere. My son Patrick was known to do any and every drug presented to him. And this life of addiction had taken such hold of him that it was all encompassing. The one and only goal in life was to get high. Of course, he had to work to provide money for his habit, but stealing worked just as well. Out of financial necessity, he did both.

So there they sat at the party, smoking pot. But this was not the main event. They were simply building up to what would come later: heroin. At forty dollars a pop, it was an expensive habit. Not everybody at this party was doing heroin, but these two buddies were all into it. Patrick's friend hadn't learned his lesson. As a result of shooting up, Bill had acquired hepatitis C.

When the time came, Bill produced a hypodermic needle. Trouble was, it was a used needle. Bill had certainly infected the hypodermic needle with the hepatitis C virus. Bill shot up and shoved the needle to Patrick.

Now it was decision time. Everything inside him was screaming for a fix. But he knew if he used Bill's needle, he would be infected with the deadly virus. Patrick took the needle and hesitated. He went for his arm and then pulled back. If he used this needle, it would affect him for the rest of his life. In fact, using this needle could possibly kill him. Did he need a fix that badly?

Patrick's childhood:
My son had been a happy child. He had a smile that would melt your heart. Patrick was upbeat and easygoing. He was an altar boy, and at the age of eight, he considered the possibility of becoming a priest. Patrick's love for God was evident in his general demeanor and in his reverence when in church. He once said that Jesus had come to him at night and had given him a Snickers bar. I never doubt such stories from children, and I did not doubt that Jesus had spoken to

Patrick. Not so coincidentally, Patrick's papa (grandfather) also used to give him Snickers bars.

There were numerous occasions when the help of Patrick's guardian angel, whom he named Michael, had certainly protected him from harm. On one such occasion in his sixth year, Patrick, wearing shorts and a T-shirt, was walking on a stone wall outside our church. Suddenly he fell from the four-foot wall into a very dense bramble-type bush having two-inch thorns. I was horrified as I raced to his aid. I had pictures in my head of horrible cuts and punctures that he had surely suffered. Prayers instinctually flooded my mind for his safety. Arriving to give him aid, I was amazed. He emerged from the bush with not one injury, not even a scratch.

Once, a man who was running for borough council stopped at our house for our signatures. Because we were friends with him, he stayed awhile as we talked on the front porch. I had to excuse myself to leave for work. He and Anne continued talking. I got into the car and started backing out of the driveway. At the same moment, Anne said good-bye, and the man stepped down from the porch. Forcefully he yelled, "*Stop!*" I hit my brakes. Patrick had emerged from behind the bushes and was pedaling across the driveway on his tricycle. I surely would have hit Patrick had there not been impeccable timing of all that transpired.

Indeed, in retrospect, it is amazing and utterly miraculous that through all of Patrick's drug use, he remained alive. Patrick's guardian angel certainly worked overtime protecting him.

Patrick was a charmer. And having been raised with many sisters, he learned the fine art of diplomacy. In my opinion, Patrick's childhood was ideal. Everything was fine and dandy. He had a wonderful relationship with both sets of grandparents. Papa was his favorite.

Anne reflects on Patrick:
> The birth of a baby is always exciting, but Patrick's was special—the first boy after all girls! He was a sweet and perpetually happy baby: not always calm, but good and very much loved! He grew steadily and fit into our family perfectly. With more sisters after him, he became Dad's ally and my "little man."

But a crisis struck in 1992 when Patrick was nine years old. His beloved papa died. Though the initial shock was severe, we assumed that in time, Patrick's wounds would heal. However, in retrospect, this event became a turning point in his life. Patrick resented God for taking away his papa. His struggle was mostly internal, but it affected his life. Eventually Patrick's grades began to slip, and he began getting into trouble at school. By the fifth grade, he began acting the drug-culture persona. I warned him that the way he acted would determine who he became, but he brushed off the warning.

Patrick's zest for life was being very slowly sucked out of him. We could see the decline but hoped that it would only be temporary. By his junior-high-school years, his behavior in school became disruptive, and his grades were worse. I believe that it was in the eighth grade that he initially experimented with drugs. Of course, marijuana was the first step.

However, not all was bad. There were many good times too. He seemed to be able to balance the two worlds in which he found himself. We have always been a very religious family. Each summer we attended what is called a Holy Family Fest at Catholic Familyland in Ohio. When immersed in this environment, he indeed thrived. He and his younger sister would go to the chapel to pray, without us even suggesting it. At this point, we were unaware of his drug use.

Though Patrick remained an altar boy, often his actions didn't reflect his former self. It was a constant game of parental strategy to remain close to him and guide him in correct actions. Outwardly, it seemed to be only normal teenage rebellion. We still didn't know of his deeper experimentation with drugs. In his senior-high-school years, our greatest concern was his loss of the sense of a need to attend church. He adopted the attitude of many so-called intellectuals. "Religion is for the weak," he would proclaim. "It is good in that it keeps the masses in line, but that's it." He claimed to be above the need for religion. And concerning God, he did feel that there was a "greater power." Despite his lack of enthusiasm for church, we insisted that as long as he lived in our house, he would have to attend Mass with us on Sundays.

I don't intend to paint a dismal picture of Patrick. He and I went through Cub Scouts and Boy Scouts together, me being the den leader and assistant scoutmaster. Patrick even attained the prestigious rank of Eagle Scout. One of our favorite activities was building models together. Several military aircraft hung from his bedroom ceiling. We had great times camping and going on family vacations. We even attended rock concerts together. He was a dear boy and young man, and quite charming. He was very humorous at times. I could see sensitivity in him. On the one hand, his feelings could be easily hurt, though he didn't show it, and on the other hand, he was much attuned to the feelings of others. He was able to empathize with them.

Patrick's senior-high-school years:
As previously stated, Patrick was very good at bridging the two worlds of family life and religion on one side of the spectrum and his drug use on the other side. He was certainly a good worker, having had a paying job for much of his life. He was very introspective. His writing and poetry were top rate. He was clever, for the good and for the bad. Patrick was ingenious, but he also determined that he was

too smart to follow all the rules that others followed. He was above that and believed that he could outsmart the system. And he did.

A couple of times, we had him consult a psychologist, and once a psychiatrist. He knew exactly what they wanted to hear and got the report from them that he desired. The psychiatrist told him that his depression stemmed from a lack of attention from his father, because I didn't encourage him to play sports. We did Boy Scouts, camping, caving, boating, and hiking; we built tree cabins, fixed his bikes together, and went to concerts. And we certainly did throw around the football and baseball as well as kick the soccer ball in the backyard. But Patrick's goal was accomplished when he was prescribed Serotonin and Wellbutrin. He was very good at getting what he wanted.

I tried to keep the communication between us an open exchange. Together, we attended a Bob Dylan concert, his favorite. We also saw the Who, as well as Roger Waters. I wanted to stay within his world. These concerts were good bonding experiences.

Anne gives her perspective:
> The years of Patrick's addiction are remembered as an emotional roller coaster. When we first became aware of his using drugs, I was filled with shock and disbelief. "How can this have happened in our family?" I loved my son dearly but was very disappointed that he had let himself become addicted to drugs. This did not fit into my plan for our family! I had the other children to think about, and I think that for a long time, I just denied the seriousness of the problem. I figured it was just a phase that Patrick was going through and that with enough love and prayers, he would be fine. I let my husband handle most of the everyday situations with Patrick and continued to care for the other children as best I could.

But in senior high, cracks in his facade began to appear. We had grave doubts that he would even graduate from high school. His grades were dismal and his attendance record threatened his graduation. In his junior year, we enrolled him in tutoring. We were surprised to learn that his reading level was that of a fifth grader. Ironically, it was in the fifth grade that Patrick's resentment of God at the death of his papa had burst out from his subconscious, externally affecting his actions. Apparently, at that point, he had just decided to stop learning. Fortunately, within a couple of months of tutoring, Patrick was reading at his proper level, and his grades improved remarkably.

Raising Patrick was a series of contrasts. There were many (excuse the expression) "highs" and numerous lows. I have quite a lot of fond memories of our time spent together. Though I love my entire family and daughters dearly, Patrick was my only son. I relished the times we spent at Seph Mack Scout Camp. I'd take him to all the spots I had trod when I was a summer-camping scout at the same place. I would regale him with stories of my scouting adventures. We were close.

Anne and I did everything we could to keep him close to us and close to God. In his teenage years, on numerous occasions, I paid him twenty dollars to go to Confession. I figured that if he at least got to the confessional, he would have a chance of obtaining grace. Later in life he told us that the first thing he would confess was that his dad was paying him to be there. And in these moments of coerced confession, there were some signal graces given to Patrick. He shared with me at the time what one priest told him: "I've never done this before, but I feel that I am being led to tell you something. I want you to know that you will lead many people to Heaven." There was a similar experience with another priest in the confessional who told him that there was much grace about him. So I did have reason for hope. But worldly matters and the craving for a high crowded out Patrick's need for God.

One day we received a call from the Rite Aid drugstore. Apparently Patrick had passed a bad check there. The story we finally dragged out of Pat was that a woman had convinced him of what we considered to be an absurd scheme. She would give him fifty dollars in cash, and he would purchase items at Rite Aid for her totaling seventy-five dollars, using his checkbook from a closed account. They did this several times before the checks bounced.

After a thorough interrogation of our son, we took him to the store to apologize to the manager and to pay back the money he owed. Of course, the money now came from my checkbook. Had Patrick not still been in high school, I wouldn't have paid this bill. But I hoped that this was a lesson that he would remember. I did, however, add this amount to a tally of what Patrick owed me. And he spent some time being grounded. At this point, we did not know that Patrick's ill-gotten gains were most likely being spent on drugs.

I was quite grateful that the store manager hadn't pressed charges. Some years later, I returned to the store and told Patrick's entire story to the manager. I again thanked him for giving my son a second chance.

Though there were setbacks in his life and battles of the will, we continued to love him completely. The more he rebelled, the more love we lavished upon him. But for some reason, at times, this had an adverse effect. In my estimation, Patrick didn't think that he deserved our love, so the more we loved him, the more he pulled away. And isn't that just the situation with our eternal destiny? God doesn't "send" anybody to hell. The separated soul chooses hell.

As we read in John 3:19–21, "This is the judgment, that the Light has come into the world, and men loved the darkness rather than the Light, for their deeds were evil. For everyone who does evil hates the Light, and does not come to the Light for fear that his deeds will be exposed. But he who practices the truth comes to the Light, so that his deeds may be manifested as having been wrought in God."

Consequently, Patrick came to love the darkness and reject the light of our love.

We used many forms of prayer methods: novenas, sacramentals, and so on. I placed a green scapular under his mattress and frequently blessed him with holy water. Our family did a fifty-four-day rosary novena for him. His siblings all prayed for him. His sister Maura used to go to Baba and Papa's grave, where she cried for Patrick and also prayed for him. At every turn we were asking people to pray for Patrick. We sought out holy people, especially priests, to ask for their prayers. Easily, there were over one hundred people praying for our son.

It is amazing that Patrick didn't end up in jail. It seemed that his friends were dropping left and right, being suspended from school, being arrested, spending time in jail, overdosing, and so on. But somehow, Patrick avoided these pitfalls. He hung out mostly with his friend Mac and his cousin Ronnie. They would get high and do stupid things in imitation of the *Jackass Show*.

Ronnie was typical of those using marijuana. He had very little motivation, and getting him out of bed in the morning was a struggle. I experienced this firsthand, because he spent some time living with us. Pot, parties, and pretty girls were all that motivated him. He was a great guy and easy to get along with, but any motivation that he might acquire was quickly taken away by the pot.

On one evening, Ronnie and Patrick decided on a new thrill. They threw a ball of string out of Pat's bedroom window and held on to one end. Then they took the ball to the garage and tied it to a gasoline can. Returning to the bedroom, they reeled in the string and hoisted the gas can to Patrick's bedroom so they could huff the gasoline there. I shudder to think of what could have happened. Most importantly, they could have been killed through the huffing, or they could have unwittingly ignited themselves. And they could have burned down the entire house, potentially incinerating the family.

On another occasion, Patrick had stolen money from a fellow user. Some days later he was walking down the street. Patrick was startled as two cars screeched to a halt and a pack of guys poured out of the vehicles. They grabbed Patrick and threw him into one of the cars. They demanded the $200 he had stolen. The gang was intent on pounding the pulp out of Patrick after he said that he didn't have any money. Some fast talking ensued as he tried to get out of this jam. Finally Patrick proffered that he could get some money at his friend's house. Arriving at the given address, Patrick said that his friend wasn't home but that he could get in through a window. With the gang surrounding him, he climbed through the window. He wasted no time in running to the back of the house and climbing out another window. He then made his escape. Who knows how bad a beating he would have gotten had he not gotten away? Again, I attribute Patrick's safety to the protection of his guardian angel.

At one point, Patrick and Mac found themselves at odds with each other. Mac accused Patrick of ratting on him during an interrogation by the high-school principal. The word got out that Patrick had ratted. An ambush was planned to pay Patrick back for his treason. Of course, Patrick claimed innocence. I found out about this because I had guessed Patrick's e-mail password. By corroborating information from his e-mail and things I heard on the street, I knew that an ambush was coming, and I knew the time and place. I couldn't let Patrick know of my hacking into his e-mail, so I arranged for him to be far away when this attack was to occur. When the guys realized that Patrick wasn't coming to the spot where they knew he'd be, they instead snuck onto my property and slashed a tire on each of my cars.

But that wasn't the end of it. Perhaps they knew that I was the one who had foiled their attack on Patrick. I had an informer in the group. Maybe the informer was playing both sides. A couple of weeks had gone by when, in the middle of the night, I heard crashes coming from outside. I saw a boy smashing the windows of my van. I threw on some clothes and was soon in hot pursuit. I followed the boy home and pounded on his door at one o'clock in the morning. His parents were not too happy at the disturbance. But they agreed to pay for the damage, so I didn't involve the police.

At times, I would secretly follow Patrick as he left the house. I discovered that one of his hangouts was behind an old creamery building where open-air concrete-walled storage areas provided Patrick and his friends some privacy, away from peering eyes.

On one occasion, Patrick was acting strange. He was very much on edge, and at the same time, he was both listless and displaying symptoms of depression. As he exited the front door, I became concerned. I wondered whether Patrick was going out to drink alcohol or do drugs, or whether he was going to commit suicide.

My worry became overpowering as a sense of dread took hold of me. I wished that I had stopped him from going out. I then decided to find him. I ran to the driveway to get the car. To my dismay, I discovered that Anne had taken one car, and my daughter had the other one.

Feeling desperation, I hopped onto my youngest daughter's two-wheeler. Problem was, this bike had fifteen-inch tires. I'm certain that I was quite a spectacle, frantically pedaling across town with all my might, standing on this tiny bicycle.

When I reached the creamery, I crept up above the cement barriers, scouting for my son. There he was. As I took in the scene, I was relieved to see that Pat and his friends were laughing. Fortunately, these teenagers were only smoking cigarettes. I was relieved to see that Patrick was happy and was not doing drugs or alcohol.

We tried in our parenting to not be over reactive but also not to be under reactive. We realized that kids go through phases, so we tried to take the long view. Would this issue really matter six months or a year from now? We especially wanted our children to know that we were approachable. If they came clean and told the truth about a matter, punishment would be less. But if they lied, we'd bring the hammer down. We faced two such issues with Patrick.

We once questioned him about some money that was missing. He fessed up that he had taken it. His punishment was to make a list of everything that he had ever stolen from us. To our surprise, the list was quite extensive.

On another occasion, in his junior-high-school years, he denied that he had done a certain misdeed. After an interrogation and extensive research on our part, we came to the conclusion that Patrick had indeed done this thing. There was no way that it was not him. When we told him that he would be punished, he began negotiating what that punishment should be. We talked about grounding him and paddling him, as well as other alternatives.

Patrick was very persuasive and a good negotiator. After some discussion, we agreed that he would receive just one smack with our wooden paddle. I took him to the garage and had him bend over. Taking aim, and with a good amount of force, I gave him three quick smacks. Astonished and indignant, he grabbed his butt and hopped up and down while saying in an accusing tone, "You said just one swat." I replied, "Now you know what it is like to be lied to." In my opinion, this was a true case of the punishment fitting the crime.

It is amazing also that Patrick was able to keep his job. Once, in about eleventh grade, he almost flipped out at work one evening. He must have been high on acid, because he said that when he opened the cash register and began counting change back to a customer, all of the money appeared as if it were Monopoly money. Try as he might, he couldn't make the money turn into real money. And yet, Patrick was highly praised by his bosses. At each job he held, they had high esteem for him and counted him as one of their best workers. How ironic!

Patrick and Ronnie were at a party. They began their routine. First came the pot. They smoked about an eighth of an ounce. Then came the mushrooms. Next they did acid. At this point, Ronnie had had enough and tried to mellow out. But not so for Patrick. He was driven to do more. He did several more hits of acid. His friends wondered why he hadn't overdosed. They tried to talk him out of doing anything else. But he wasn't done yet. He then moved on to cocaine. He did a couple of lines and wanted more. There was talk about calling an ambulance for him, but everyone was afraid of being arrested. Patrick was calling for anything and everything that could get him higher. But his friends made him stop. With the amount of drugs he had done, it seemed like a miracle that Patrick hadn't died that night.

Considering the number of close calls from which he had escaped, it seemed like he was being kept alive for a reason. But for what unseen purpose? Only time would tell.

As things deteriorated, Patrick became more determined that religion was only for the weak. He believed that religion was essential to society in that it helped maintain good order, but he was adamant that he was above all of that and didn't need religion.

Several times throughout his school career, we garnered support from our children. We would jointly engage in a novena, with special prayers being said each day for nine days. To the younger ones, this was just Mom and Dad praying more prayers. Perhaps the older children realized that these prayers were needed for their brother.

Patrick's young adulthood:
After barely graduating from high school, Patrick enrolled in a computer technical school. Unbeknownst to us, the majority of his time in Pittsburgh was not spent at school. Though he lived in the school dormitory, in his first semester he missed over half of his classes. In a short time, he withdrew from school, leaving us with the bill.

As Patrick's bad situation became worse, we overcame our shame. Too often, parents hide their child's addiction because they feel it reflects badly upon their parenting skills, or they avoid disclosure simply out of embarrassment. Finally, we broke our silence and revealed to our parents this dire situation. We then included them in our special prayers, such as the fifty-four-day rosary novena, with a rosary being prayed each of those days for our special intention.

Despite his destructive behavior, Patrick always had a way of bouncing back. (Perhaps the result of all of those prayers being said for him). He took a summer job at Cedar Point. He met a nice girl, and they became engaged. Amazingly, she became Catholic at Patrick's prompting. My wife, Anne, and I are Rachael's godparents. Patrick obtained a good job at a hospital in another state. He received high recommendations and was put on the fast track for promotion. Things seemed to be going his way. We were overjoyed that he had escaped the grasp of drugs and had again embraced his faith.

I received a glimpse into Patrick's inner thoughts when one of my daughters suggested that I read his blogs that he had published openly online.

Patrick blogged:
>Confusion swirls up and down,
>As thoughts of the past go round and round.
>Memories make me sick, as I enter the night,
>I try to forget, I try to fight.
>Make it all stop, make it go away.
>Make all the night time turn into day.
>Like a bottle I fill up fast,
>Now I'm too full, my limit is passed.
>I can't live for me so I'll live for you,
>I can't promise myself so I'll give you that too.
>Maybe I'm sick, maybe I'm crazy,
>All of these memories seem so hazy.
>Up ahead I see light, I'm starting to turn,
>I see her face, as my eyes start to burn.
>I walk now slowly, not to go to her too soon,
>Her heart is the sun, and mine is the moon.
>Her starlit eyes look back to mine,
>Nothing I can say, I'm frozen in time.
>I know it will all be okay,
>I know tomorrow is another day,
>Walking with her by my side,
>Everything to tell and nothing to hide.

Rachael was a sweet girl. She seemed to be just what Patrick needed to get onto the right path. We now found ourselves in the midst of planning our fourth wedding. The past heartaches faded away. We hoped and prayed that this change in him would be permanent.

Even though Patrick was in love and was living a good life, the relentless monster of addiction would again have its way with him. Patrick was caught stealing drugs from the hospital and was promptly fired. Patrick's likable personality was probably the reason the hospital never filed charges. He was very good at making friends, and many people cared about his future. Despite the obvious lesson learned in losing his job, the evil of drug addiction was not finished with him. It also cost him his fiancée.

Patrick blogged:
>I walk all alone now, nothing can make me okay,
>I just wanna run fast, and forget about today.
>Some say actions speak louder than words, but they're all fools,
>Nice people get trampled on, that is just the rules.
>I gave it my all, but could I've done more,
>I knocked real hard, but she never opened the door.
>Stolen emotions ripped from my heart,
>I'm lying in a pile, I've fallen apart.
>Hearing all those words, hurt me deep inside,
>Something inside of me feels like it has died.
>I would give anything to make it all not true,
>But I have done what I can, there is nothing left to do.
>Hope is all I hold now, and I am holding real tight,
>I long for her lips, her touch, anything to make me feel right.
>I can't bear to think that I've kissed her for the last time,
>And that I can't tell people that she is all mine.
>There's a hole in my heart, where she once stood,
>It was there before she came, but she filled it really good.

Patrick's escape:
Patrick had run out of options in this locale. He was unemployed, and he was no longer engaged. Additionally, he had narrowly escaped serious legal troubles at the hospital where he had worked. Patrick needed to get away, but he did not want to return to his hometown.

He then asked his sister if he could move in with her and her family. Autumn and her husband, Miguel, lived in a rural western state, which to Patrick was an ideal situation. He would be far away from the troubles that he had recently created. And he would be away from the troubles he'd escaped from in his hometown. Additionally, Patrick would be living with family.

This change actually did Patrick lots of good. He regularly attended church with the family and made many friends. At one point, Patrick attended a faith-building retreat at the parish. This experience kindled in him a desire to live a more faith-filled life. He joined a home-faith community group and was growing by leaps and bounds. He became quite close to one particular girl in the group, and she too had developed an interest in him. Eve and Patrick, while not officially dating, saw quite a lot of each other.

Patrick also developed a good relationship with a priest who lived in the area. Fr. Leonard often had Patrick over for dinner and offered him some spiritual direction as well as an occasional job.

Feeling recovered while living with Autumn and Miguel, Patrick had a scare with melanoma. He wrote a two-page e-mail to his parents and siblings. His letter read, in part:

Dear Family,

I want to thank each of you for your continued prayers and support. [He continued with a description of his melanoma prognosis, etc.]

I relish, at this point, sharing with you where I am in my spiritual journey. I have been attending a great parish. But mostly I just attended Mass with Autumn and Miguel, and did not get much out of the experience. I just went through the motions. I had been troubled in recent years about what it means to be a Catholic. As I mentioned, I wasn't getting any spiritual feeling out of Mass…

Two weeks ago I started attending a Returning Catholics class on Thursday nights…After only two sessions, I am already beginning to see The Truth that has been knocking on my heart for years. I am also looking forward to a weekend Evangelization Retreat. I can see now that it is true that you must serve others before you can serve yourself. I can see, too, that until I accept Jesus's Body and Blood as just that: I have no life in me. [See John 6:53]

It just seems to me that when I opened my heart to God, He really gave me the tools to aid me to unite my heart with His Heart. I really want to follow His plan for my life. Finally, I have the courage to ask God what he wants me to do…

It feels sometimes that I am stuck in the generation of instant gratification. I have lived my life for instant thrills. Putting a drug into my body gave me a temporary thrill, but it didn't last…I've wasted hours watching TV, along with doing other worthless things…It is hard to find people in my generation who are willing to work for what they desire…

I believe with God's help I can break that cycle in me and work hard to get where God wants me to be. I feel amazing things happening every day. Before I allowed God back into my heart, I was numb. Being addicted, I lost my friends, I lost my fiancé, and I lost my self-respect. The sense of not caring about myself overwhelmed me. I thought that I'd never be able to be happy again…I've gotten my first sense of mortality. I have come to realize that this is not the person I want to be when I meet my Maker.

At first, I blamed God for my melanoma. Then I began to see God's providence in it all. It was because of that illness, and the way it was discovered, that I came to see His actions in my life. Praise the Lord and His mysterious ways.

With love, Patrick

The uniqueness of the melanoma discovery was because the diagnosis had come because he had had an injury, which he greatly lamented at the time. But it was through visiting the doctor for this ailment, that the melanoma was discovered. The inspiration for this letter was triggered by an experience during Mass when Patrick began seeing things differently, and actually cried during the service. This spiritual experience, coupled with the realization of his mortality, moved Patrick to share these things with his family. Additionally, this turn of events indeed moved him closer to God.

His melanoma was treated by removing the affected parts of his skin and it seemed that all was well with him.

Everything was coming together in a good way. Patrick had left his troubles behind. He had a home, and he enjoyed the time with his sister, brother-in-law, and niece. He had many friends and one special friend in Eve. Patrick was involved in church activities, and he was employed at a Salvation Army thrift shop. And of utmost importance, he was free of illegal drugs. Patrick was also attending Narcotics Anonymous (NA) meetings. What could go wrong?

One day, while unloading a truck at work, Patrick fell from the loading dock. He hurt his back and needed to see a doctor. The injury wasn't too serious, but the doctor prescribed pain medication for Patrick.

It seemed that this event fractured the idyllic life he had been living. Unbeknownst to others at the time, this prescription of Vicodin ignited a suppressed desire to once again get high.

Autumn soon began noticing that she wasn't keeping very good track of her money. What she thought she had in her purse, or what might have been lying on the counter, would disappear. And there were things missing from the house, such as DVDs. It wasn't very long before it was obvious that Patrick was stealing. Autumn realized that stealing is a telltale sign of drug use.

Autumn and Miguel confronted Patrick, but he met them with denials. They attempted to help him through this failure, but his offensive behavior worsened.

Things came to the point that Autumn felt she needed to warn Eve. She exposed Patrick's recent actions to Eve and advised her not to fall in love with him. This was sound advice, for Patrick was again spiraling out of control. He began visiting hospital emergency rooms, feigning pain in the hopes of being prescribed painkillers. His stealing expanded to taking things from other people's homes where he happened to be a guest. His emergency-room bills mounted, and he experienced some scrapes with the law.

Though he had firm intentions of reform, his old ways had returned. Realizing that she was enabling Patrick's destructive behavior, his sister made the tough decision to withdraw her support. He would have to find another place to live. Patrick had worn out his welcome.

For a while, Patrick lived at a homeless shelter. Then Fr. Leonard took him in. Yet, Patrick knew that he had to get out of town.

With his departure pending, Patrick was involved in a traffic accident that landed him in jail. His NA sponsor paid Patrick's bail money with the understanding that it would eventually be paid back. But Patrick skipped town, leaving Larry with the bail/bond debt.

Patrick returns home:
Patrick moved back home with us and drowned his sorrows in more intense drug use. He was doing heroin, LSD, every type of pill, and anything else he could beg, buy, or steal.

A look at a few of Patrick's blogs gives a glimpse of his drug-induced mind-set.

> The Hole
> There is a hole, where someone should be.
> A hole in my heart, deep inside of me.
> Who will fill this, who will care?
> Someone please try me, if you dare.
> But when you get close, and you see who I am;
> you will be running away, as fast as you can.
> You will find out, why I'm me.
> Then you will know, I'm not where you want to be.
> But I know someone will stay.
> Someone will love me 'til my last day.
> When I find you, be prepared.
> I want to meet you.

I want to know you.
I want to hold you. Forever!

<u>Hide!</u>
Button up your lip.
And don't let your shield slip.
(Take a fresh grip on your feelings-proof mask).
And if with their questions they try, to break down your disguise
You can hide behind your mask, with your own two eyes.
Put on your brave face and slip over the road where you've gone too far.
Putting on a grin as you casually lean on the bar.
Laughing inside at the rest of the world of the faces in the crowd.
You hide behind petrified eyes in a world gone wild.
Don't believe in their stories of fame, fortune and glory.
Or you'll be caught in a haze of this evil age, it's their story.
The pie-in-the-sky turned out to be miles too high.
So hide behind those brown and mild eyes. Oh why?

His other blogs contained lines such as these:
    I'm all sucked dry, down to the very last breath.
    Someone, what is wrong with me?
    It is true I've been beaten down to death…

    If I show you my dark side, will you still hold me tonight?
    If I open my heart to you, show you my weak side—What would you do?

Patrick had dug himself into a hole. His self-worth was dismal. Though we offered him love, his drugs and his moral confusion caused him to repel that offering. He could see nothing beyond the shroud of his strung-out and damaged psyche.

Patrick's fateful decision:
Let us now return to Patrick's party with Bill. Patrick was facing a fateful decision. Would he use a hepatitis C–infected needle, or would he reject Bill's offer?

Bill shot up with heroin and shoved the infected needle to Patrick. A battle raged in Patrick's mind. Everything inside him was screaming for a fix. But he knew if he used Bill's needle, he would be infected with the deadly virus. Using this needle would affect him for the rest of his life. In fact, using this needle could kill him. Hepatitis C does not go away. Did he need a fix that badly?

Patrick took the needle and hesitated. He went for his arm and then pulled back. Ultimately, his bodily craving for heroin overpowered any sense of right judgment that he might have had. Patrick thrust the needle into his vein. The heroin began coursing through his body, bringing elation. And the hepatitis C was coursing through his body as well. Long after this high was over, the hepatitis would remain. And from that day forward, he was plagued with the symptoms of this deadly disease.

Patrick blogged:
>I stick a needle in my arm,
>Why do I do my body such harm,
>'Cause everythin' in me cries for a fix,
>Doesn't matter what's in it, just give me a mix.
>I'm shootin' up at half past eleven,
>The feelin' I get, is this what it's like in heaven,
>Nothing's wrong in the world as I lay in a stupor,
>I'm in my own world and it feels kinda super,
>This drug has me under a hypnotic spell,
>This ain't heaven, I think its hell.

Patrick's life was a wreck. He knew that he needed to get clean but was unable to summon the courage to deal with it. Parental begging and pleading finally won out as he agreed to be admitted at Gateway Rehabilitation Center.

Patrick's drug-use autobiography:
This tragic saga I've told is also told by my son. Patrick wrote the following while attending rehab at Gateway.

[With the aim of keeping this book family friendly, Patrick's expletives have been replaced with symbols].

His testimony is as follows:
> Ever since I was young, I remember wondering what drugs felt like. I wondered: What does that beer do to my uncles and aunts at family events? What do cigarettes taste like? Why do people do it, and why do they seem so silly and happy?
>
> About 1996 I was twelve years old, and I listened to the Beatles a lot. As I learned about them, marijuana seemed to be the driving force as to why they were so cool. At that point, I didn't know about the LSD they did. But I still thought a lot about trying pot.
>
> One day, this kid Nate, who I had a paper route with, told me he had some pot to sell. Instantly I said that I wanted some. So I broke my sister's piggy bank and bought an eighth of an ounce.
>
> It's funny because literally ten minutes after he gave it to me, I was alone in the woods trying pot for the first time, by myself. That first time, I didn't really feel high.

As time went on, I turned many of my friends on to it, and soon enough, we were smoking pot on the regular and drinking my friend's mom's boxed wine.

My other friend Bob would have us over often, and we would have our way with his dad's Crown Royal! I remember getting sick often at the time. We thought it was funny.

All of us smoked cigarettes too at that time. So we just thought we were the cat's @#$ for our adult-like behaviors we partook in. I guess that was how adults enjoyed themselves.

Around the same time, the same kid Nate sold me some opium. Instantly, the ball rolled from there. I was willing to try anything just to see its effects.

As I experimented more, I lost a lot of my friends, because I was more extreme, I guess. They made the right move, though. I hung out with the potheads. By tenth grade, all my friends were the people I got high with. We were just skating through life in one big haze of smoke.

In 2000, when I was in the tenth grade, I started experimenting with ecstasy. I would take it nearly every day. I was what they call E-tarded. At the same time, I found acid as well.

As with all the drugs I experimented with, I took acid and E to the extreme. I would take ten hits at a time and stack three E pills on top. I can't say too much about that period because I still feel like it changed my brain too much, and I don't like to revisit those thoughts.

My best friend, Cathie, had a boyfriend, Gravely, and I would get high at his place every day before work. Her brother was a big hookup, and we would steal a lot of his best weed.

One day we found a bag of weed that had a lot of white on it. Thinking it was THC, I smoked it. It turned out to be PCP, and to say the least, I was nuts. Every sound was the police. I hid from everyone because I felt like they were in on something against me.

Cathie would also get us a lot of hash, so we smoked quite a bit of that too. I remember smoking weed dipped in embalming fluid with her too. Mushrooms were my favorite treat she acquired for us. We would get out of our minds eating 'shrooms.

As I started eleventh grade, I hung out with my friend Mac more and more. We were in the same grade, and we both smoked weed. But it wasn't long until we did harder drugs.

I got my wisdom teeth pulled that year and was prescribed Vicodin. My friend Dirk's mom tried to buy them from me, so I knew that they would mess me up. Hence, I finished the bottle in a matter of days.

At that time, Dirk's mom was getting scripts for OxyContin (OC) from Dr. Mirro. On the fifteenth of each month, she would give myself, Dirk, and Mac all we needed until they were gone. Needless to say, I was in love. His mom, Betty, also smoked crack. But at the time, I wouldn't try it.

Mac and I started helping this kid slang E, so we were making money. Every now and then, we would help him count his cash and pocketed four to five hundred dollars apiece. We were dealing with tens of thousands of dollars, so it went minorly unnoticed.

Then my friend and I robbed another dealer one day. We got $20,000, and there was no way anybody could suspect us. That is when I found cocaine (blow).

Mac and I spent over $20,000 in one month on coke and OCs. I did it in school, at home, basically everywhere. I remember that one time I stayed awake for seven days. I was such a wreck.

At that same time, Mac and I started getting rid of blow to support our habits. We would get a ball, sell a few grams for a ridiculous amount, and blow our profits—literally.

I had an accident that summer that left me with a lot of back pain. My doctor was giving me sixty Lortab 10s every ten days. I also got Soma from the same doctor.

I stopped using coke because I preferred the pills. But still I experimented quite a bit. Cathie invited me to a festival where I tried peyote and Ketamine in a three-day period, Special K, as they call it. It really messed me up. I had an out-of-body experience that really freaked me out!

My senior year in high school started. By that time, I was using every day. Either OxyContin, Soma, Lortab, or Xanax. I couldn't go to school unless I was @#$%^& up. I would even smoke weed every day after lunch in school.
My friends were getting a lot of benzo-type drugs at the time. Ativan, Klonopin, and Valium just to name a few. I remember taking Ativan with Mac. We robbed my friend and

didn't even remember doing it. I just woke up with a bunch of his stuff in my house.

Once I graduated, I moved to Forbes Avenue in Pittsburgh. That is where I met heroin. I wasn't getting my regular @#$%, so it seemed to be a great substitute. It was dirt cheap, and I could get a lot of it.

Well, that was short-lived. I dropped out of school in the Burg and went back home.

Betty, my friend's mom, took me under her wing and showed me crack. My OC hookup was back, and we were cooking up crack to get even more @#$%^& up. That is when I really went deep.

I illegally started getting money out of my trust fund to support my habit. To date, I'd spent almost $300,000 on my habits. It was madness. Eventually, my relationship with Betty and Dirk fizzled, and I was all pills again. Every ten days, seeing good old Dr. Mirro.

[Dr. Mirro is currently serving a term in federal prison for providing drugs to his patients. Patrick's trust fund eventually needed to be liquidated in order to pay off his numerous debts.]

My girlfriend, Chrissy, at the time was a user too, and she was never happy with just my scripts. So we would travel to Pittsburgh every other day to pick up dope. That is when I started putting needles into my arm.

Four months later, my girlfriend and I broke up, and I had had enough of my hometown. I wanted to get clean but couldn't do it there. So I got a job at Cedar Point in Ohio. I just straight-up left town.

That is where I met Rachael. She is my former fiancée. But I will try not to write too much about her. (It was too painful of an experience to lose her).

Man, that summer I was generally clean. No weed, almost no pills, other than the two times I went to the emergency room (ER) and got some Lortab. I was in love! Life was great. Life was so great that I moved to another state to continue my relationship with Rachael. I got a job at Hall Memorial Hospital and worked hard as hell. Then the pain in my back returned.

I was almost a year into being there when my doctor put me on Vicodin ES. And so the ball rolled again. I was straight-up addicted as @#$% again. I even went to another doctor on the side for two years who gave me Valium, Soma, and Ultram every two weeks.

Rachael eventually caught on, and I went to outpatient rehab. That worked for a few weeks; then I filled my scripts again. It was then that I decided that, out of love for Rachael, I would quit drugs, cold turkey. And I did. Yet I still took the Valium and Soma. I thought that opiates were my only problem.

I ended up getting seizures from too much Soma and was eventually hospitalized. I scared everyone but didn't reveal the reason it had happened.

[At this news, we rushed across two states to see Patrick. He told us that he'd had the seizures due to a bump on the head when he fell from an exercise machine. And we believed it.]

> Around that time, I found a way to steal meds from the hospital where I worked. I took it all. If it was an opiate, I would steal it.
>
> This went on for months, until I got too scared and quit my job in fear of getting caught. I had to tell Rachael I had been lying to her, and she left me. We were to be married that June, but she could not marry a liar.
>
> I moved back home and wanted to clean myself up. I put it off and started doing drugs again. I also went to a Methadone clinic as well. But I just did that for a buzz.
>
> I realize now that I was incapable of loving Rachael because I didn't love myself. Look at what I was doing to my body! I am tired of telling her I will change. So now I will do it.
>
> On a Monday, I got a script of Vicodin, and by Friday I decided to come to Gateway. I do this for me and for all the people I have hurt through my addiction. I realize that I will never be happy as an addict. I will change!

It was at Gateway that Patrick penned the following:

> To my addiction—
> After almost nine long years, it is time to say good-bye. Before I can leave you to rest, there are some words I must say to you. @#$% you, addiction. You have brought me nothing but pain. Sure, you made it seem fun in the beginning, but every time I was vulnerable, you stuck out

your vile head. @#$% you for letting me hurt the ones I love. I wish for you to not affect me negatively again in any way. Today I kill you. You no longer have a hold over me. You can try to sneak back up on me, but I am now strong to your evil ways. You told me I didn't deserve love; you told me I wasn't @#$%. Well, @#$%^&, you aren't @#$%. I will not succumb to your tricks. You offered me happiness and delivered pain. You deceived me into thinking I couldn't be myself without you. But now I see that you wanted me to stay by myself, so I could live in solitude with you. I lost my fiancée to you. So I say, dead you will remain. Why did I choose you over Rachael, my family, and my integrity? You are nothing but false hope and a quick fix to a bigger problem. With you I felt nothing. You broke me and made me numb. Now I feel again, and for the greatest part, I feel hatred for you. Yes, I created you, but that means I can also destroy you. You will not control me again! I will never believe your lies. I will always remember the pain that you have to offer. My friends, family, and acquaintances never saw you. You hid well within me. Now, your ugly @#$ comes out of me, and everyone can see the true me again. I know you are scared as @#$%^&*# of Gateway, for they have the tools to end you. That is why I now finally tell you that you are not my friend. You are not my hope. You are not my happiness. You are not my emotions. And foremost, you are not me. So good-bye, addiction. I hope you rot in the worst pit of hell.

With all my hate and rage, Patrick

Anne remembers well these difficult and trying times.
> When Patrick was a patient at Gateway Rehab, I finally had to confront my feelings of disappointment and anger. I vividly remember attending a group session with other

parents and addicts. I listened but couldn't verbalize the pain I felt. I started out thinking that these other people were not like us—they don't have strong families with faith in God. But the more I listened, the more I saw people who were just like us—good parents who were mystified by the addiction of their sons and daughters.

Each night Patrick was away, I would pray that God would heal him and everything would be okay. Patrick was assuring us that he was done with the drugs and that he would be fine once he got home. He swore to attend the Narcotics Anonymous meetings and stay clean. He expressed plans to go to school and continue his life. I clung to the hope that he was being honest and that all would indeed be well.

Patrick's writing at Gateway is quite an impressive diatribe against his addiction. He is obviously very serious and sincere in his desire to escape the quicksand of addiction. Has he finally reached the beginning of the end of his addiction? Time will tell. Stay tuned.

To recap Patrick's addictive spiral, below I have created a listing, though not exhaustive, of the drugs that Patrick has abused throughout the years. They are listed more or less in the order of their first use. As is evident here, marijuana is most certainly a gateway drug. This is almost exclusively the first drug experimented with for those who go on to do harder drugs.

Patrick's first illegal substance abuse was alcohol. This was followed by marijuana and hash. Looking for a different thrill, he began huffing gasoline. Still seeking a higher high, Patrick turned to ecstasy, acid, THC, PCP, and LSD. And in a morbid turn, he experimented with smoking marijuana laced with embalming fluid. This use was followed by eating peyote mushrooms and using cocaine. His list of prescription pills used illegally is quite lengthy.

Patrick abused his body by ingesting OxyContin, Vicodin, Lortab, Soma, Ketamine, Xanax, numerous benzo-type drugs, Ativan, Klonopin. Ultram, Serotonin and Wellbutrin. He followed a common pattern among drug users: once the pill use becomes prohibitively expensive, they turn to a less expensive alternative. Patrick's next step in this ever-increasing search for a high led to his use of heroin. He started smoking heroin, and eventually he turned to injecting this deadly drug.

The adverse side effects of these drugs do not even begin to tell the whole story. An overdose of any one of these drugs can be fatal. And their interactions when taken together are quite unpredictable. There are also the psychological as well as physiological addictions associated with each drug. These factors, along with the often immature, reckless, impulsive, and thoughtless actions of a teenager, make that user extremely vulnerable to arrest, accidents, and death. Add to this the fact that the teenager is in a mind-altered state, and the probability of some disaster occurring is nearly certain.

After numerous years of poisoning his body with these substances, Patrick resolved to put it all behind him. After several weeks at Gateway, he returned home to us. Reading such a testimony of Patrick speaking to his addiction, one would reasonably surmise that he would never again abuse drugs. He acted confident. And we were hopeful.

Well, as the Gospel tells us, "The spirit is willing, but the flesh is weak." Though he had good intentions, it was not long before Patrick was doing drugs again. He was in a ruinous state.

In years past, Patrick had tried numerous detox and treatment centers. We learned later that often users agree to go to these centers just because they need a break from the drugs. Many have no intentions of ever changing; they just need a vacation. We also learned that when Patrick attended Narcotics Anonymous (NA), he found his best dealer connections there. Speaking with drug users lately, I've found that it is their opinion that NA needs to segregate their meetings so that the new and usually young attendees don't mix with the older ones, nor with those that are court-ordered to attend. Many drug addicts with whom I've spoken have recommended that young addicts seeking help attend Alcoholics Anonymous (AA) rather than NA. Patrick also found new dealers for himself while in various treatment centers.

Patrick blogged:
>Today is just an endless day,
>My bed seems so far away.
>I lay down in it, try to get some rest,
>Still no sleep, my sanity's getting a test.
>My body is tired, my mind it aches,
>My fingers hurt, my body shakes.
>All alone, no one to hold,
>The room is hot, but I'm still cold.
>Why won't my mind stop thinking?
>Why do I keep on sinking?
>I would give up anything for some sleep.
>But my thoughts have run way too deep.
>I want out, I need somebody here,
>As soon as my friends are gone my thoughts are near.
>Tomorrow won't come unless I slumber,
>At least for me, and this spell that I'm under.

Things were at their worst as our family prepared for our yearly trip to Catholic Familyland. This year, due to his job, Patrick would not be joining us. He was living at home, but we knew that we couldn't trust him to be in our home without us. So we set up a bed and food for him in our detached garage. He'd have to spend the week eating and sleeping there.

I locked up the house and set out for Ohio. It wasn't more than a couple of days before we got a phone call from our neighbor. The police were at our house and shouting at people in the attic windows. We didn't know what to think.

Eventually I was able to speak with a policeman. We determined that it was our son, Patrick, in the house, but we didn't know the identity of the other two people. We told the officer that Patrick was permitted to be there. We were on pins and needles for the rest of the week until we got home.

When we arrived home, we learned from Patrick what had transpired. Patrick had gotten a ladder from our garage and climbed to an upper window to gain entry into the house. He then did what many kids do when their parents aren't home. He had a party.

But after the party, his friend Dirk and Dirk's mother, Betty, refused to leave. They decided that they would take up residence in the attic and cook up some crack. Our neighbor took notice of all of the commotion at our house and called the police.

Once home, we spent quite some time collecting the burned spoons, makeshift pipes, and other drug paraphernalia from our house. We were disgusted with these events. And we were quite mystified as to why a mother and her son would be doing crack together.
As an aside, during our cleanup, I found a Polaroid photo of Betty and Dirk. I pinned the picture to the wall in the back of our garage. And every time I pass that photograph, I say a prayer for the two of them. Their photo remains there to this day.

Anne doesn't even like to think about this harrowing event.
> It was the summer that we were at our vacation at Catholic Familyland—the summer that we got the phone call from the police, that I hit my emotional low point. I couldn't speak…I

could barely think. As we walked into our home that had been violated by "drug addicts," I just kept wandering around in shock. How could our son have done this to us? He brought in strangers and let them live in our home, sleep in our beds, and use our things! I was angry, scared, and numb. At this point, my reaction internalized and I began to get sick with colitis. I also withdrew from the youth ministry I was involved in at our church. How could I help other teenagers when my own son was ruined? I felt worthless as a parent and doubted that I had anything to share. I know now that my feelings of guilt were not helping anyone, but I was caught up in my own despair.

Our other children were suffering too, but we were so wrapped up in Patrick's problems and the hope of success, that I think we may have overlooked their pain. My physical problems continued as I had stomach issues often. I shut down as far as talking to anyone about what was going on in our family. For Patrick's sake and ours, I tried to pretend that everything was fine. If anyone inquired about Patrick, I would just say, "He's doing better now." I guess I thought saying it might make it true.

The tension in our household was teeming with fear, disappointment, and hopelessness. How could we get through to our son the necessity of getting clean? He was slipping away, and it seemed that we could do nothing about it.

Patrick blogged:
What to reach for next, for what to stride,
What to believe in, to which should I abide.
Where should I reach for the hope that I'm seekin'.
Who's gonna fill the hole in my heart that is leakin'.
I'm waitin' for someone to inspire me to be great,

I thought I had it all, but now it's too late.
Who's gonna wake me up from my metaphorical sleep,
Who's gonna fill the position that no one else could keep.
When do I start to really come alive.
When's the next time my heart will take a dive.
I am all alone and will stay this way,
Until we meet again someday.
But if we meet again, and introduced as friends,
Please don't let on that you knew me when.
I was lonely and close to the end.

It was at this time that Patrick had his first drug-related arrest. The pretense for questioning him was loitering, or something benign, but a search of his pockets found a small amount of marijuana and some drug paraphernalia. Under the law, even a plastic sandwich bag, often used to hold pot, can be considered paraphernalia. He was charged with possession and went before the district magistrate. We didn't have the money for an attorney; nor did he. So the public defender took his case. Patrick incurred a $350 fine, and that was it.

His only other local scrape with the law, as far as I am aware, was some years earlier when he and his friends decided to throw snowballs out of their car windows. The officer who stopped them accused them of discharging missiles from a moving vehicle. He handcuffed the group of four and read them the riot act. I believe he only wanted to scare them, because after taking them to the police station, he let them go. This experience cost Patrick a very good friend. Sherry, a straight-A student, had done several paintings for Patrick and liked him very much. But the reality of being handcuffed made her realize that she was hanging out with the wrong crowd. Sherry ended their relationship. This loss was very hard on Patrick.

Patrick blogged:
> My time is up, my fingers froze up,
> My mouth says nothing, it is glued shut,
> I'm so alone and getting cold,
> This kinda sadness is getting old,
> I wanna die 'cause I have nothing good,
> I'll never be happy like I should,
> Nothing will satisfy this desire,
> No one will bring me up any higher,
> It's pathetic that I wanna end it all,
> But my reasons for living have grown small,
> I hope I can just bear through until tomorrow,
> Maybe that'll be the day I have no sorrow,
> If I leave I am sorry to the ones I love,
> I just hope push never comes to shove,
> I hope nothing sets me off the edge,
> And knocks me down from this tiny ledge.

Patrick has described the heroin high as being one hundred times more intense than a sexual climax. The addiction is such that earthly efforts have little chance of stemming the craving for this drug. Though Gateway did a commendable job affecting Patrick's rationality, his self-image, and his self-preservation, it was short-lived. Patrick needed something more. He needed something to transcend all these earthly attempts to cure him. He needed something very different, something untapped in his attempts to get clean. An essential element was missing.

Meanwhile things were spiraling out of control. Patrick had stolen much of my coin collection and cashed it in for face value at the bank. He stole the water jug where we had been dumping our loose change for the past five years in the hope of financing a vacation. He forged checks and withdrew money from my credit-union account. Seeing that our vacation money was gone proved to be the last straw.

I had had enough. I lured Patrick into our backyard under some false premise. I then put him into a headlock and punched him in the face several times. He did not even resist. Patrick knew that he deserved the punishment. This was the only time in his life that I had inflicted this type of punishment on him. And it gave me no satisfaction.

It was obvious to me that I too was out of control. Something had to change. Following that altercation, I began attending NA meetings with Patrick.

After a while, he became the NA treasurer. Arriving home one evening, he had a portable safe, which he said was for NA funds. The next day, feeling suspicious, I investigated the safe. Fumbling with the dial, I managed to enter the correct combination and opened the safe door. To my utter amazement, it was full of marijuana. I promptly confiscated it and returned the safe to its prior state. I didn't know quite what to do with the pot, so I hid it among my diabetes supplies—a place he would never look.

When Patrick discovered my heist, he bewailed me with complaints. He told me of how he owed money for that pot and needed to sell it to pay the money back. And if he didn't pay, he'd be in real trouble. His life might be in danger. I considered paying that debt with my own money, but it became unnecessary.

Patrick had found the stash in my diabetes supplies. What I didn't realize was that he regularly visited my supplies in order to get hypodermic needles for his habit.

Would this nightmare ever end?

Anne was hurting too, more than I realized.
> The months and years between that first rehab time and his entering Cenacolo are a blur to me. I knew in my mind that

he was back in trouble, but I just wanted to believe that it was temporary and he would be healed. Praying for his healing was my first and only concern as I attended daily Mass. I saw him, but couldn't accept that he might still be on drugs. I only saw what I wanted to see.

I think my husband knew that my emotions were fragile, and he shielded me from the worst of it. But near the end, I could deny no longer. I still remember when I went to the ATM to take out some cash. A message came up that we were overdrawn and could not access any money. I stood there stunned and overcome with fear that Patrick had used my card and taken our money. That was confirmed when I got home and later got the bank statement. Still, Patrick explained it away and assured me that it would never happen again. But it did, as well as money disappearing from my purse and around the house. My hopes were dashed and I again fell into despair.

Patrick's life was in chaos, and everyone surrounding him experienced their own turmoil. There were expulsions from school, arrests, car accidents, attempted suicides, overdoses. His friends were falling around him. And we were falling too.

Patrick's siblings were also suffering. His sister Sally shared the following account.

> I remember a time in particular when Patrick freaked out on my parents and ran outside and mom was very upset and told us, "Everyone just please pray for Patrick!" In retrospect I really wish more would have been explained to me when I was younger. We knew there was a lot of drama and something bad was happening, but from what I remember, my parents never discussed with us what the issue was.

As I got older, I realized more of what was happening and prayed for Patrick, but it for sure seemed hopeless. I didn't think he could ever change. I wanted my fun brother back that I knew in the days before drugs, but I really didn't think he was ever coming back.

Our home was very stressful for me with all the yelling and other chaos surrounding Patrick. Also, we had a big family, so already getting not very much attention, add to that one family member who everyone is focused on constantly and it all made me feel not very important or valued in the family. Of course I have to mention our family did do many fun things and I do have a lot of good memories, but also things were very stressful growing up in a house where Patrick was always the center of all attention. It was also annoying and a bit scary when he would steal money from family members. We had to be ingenious in where we hid our money, so that our brother would not find it.

Despite his own troubles, Patrick still ministered to his fellow users. One girl in particular was very close to suicide. Patrick wrote a message to her. Perhaps he was also writing to himself.

Patrick blogged:
    Just a minute before you leave me,
    Just a minute before you shut life's door.
    What is it that you're trying to achieve here,
    Do you think we can talk about it some more?
    Please don't die on me tonight,
    I just don't think that I could handle it.
    Don't fall apart on me tonight.
    Keep your candle of hope lit.
    Yesterday's just a memory,
    Tomorrow is never what it's planned to be,

> Gut jumping isn't gonna set you free.
> I'll still be here, and the family will be too,
> I'll still be thinking, thinking about you.
> Talking about your problems, telling me 'cause you care,
> Just makes me think that it should be me standing up there.
> I can share your pain remember,
> I went through it too,
> Just not at the same time,
> But I feel just like you.
> Just don't fall apart on me now,
> 'Cause I'll fall right beside,
> Don't kill yourself sis,
> I need you to survive.

On one occasion, Patrick's friends were gathered for another party. Dave was doing Butrans painkiller patches. He applied several to himself. His last words before passing out were these: "Go out and get some more beer." Passing out was not a rare occurrence with this group, so nobody was worried about Dave. Everyone left for the beer run. Upon returning with their supplies for the evening, they found Dave still unconscious. In fact, Dave was dead.

A couple of volunteers (not Patrick) took Dave's body to the hospital. Their car screeched to a halt. They took the body from the car and left Dave on the sidewalk in front of the emergency room. And they sped away. The two were later apprehended. As far as I know, this shocking event did not deter any of the group from using drugs in the future. Everybody thinks, "It can't happen to me."

These many years of slowly losing my son to drugs were approaching a breaking point. I was at my wits' end. Patrick's return home after his firing from the hospital was indeed a low point. He had lost a promising career and had lost the love of his life. Though he could see the destructive impact of his drug use, he continued to use at an ever-increasing rate. He was drowning himself in drugs. Patrick would drag himself home at night, half dead. He had one foot in the grave. There seemed to be no hope that he would ever recover from addiction. He was lost, and I was spent.

Patrick's recovery:
I remember the day, indeed, the very moment that things changed. I had just completed St. Louis de Montfort's Total Consecration to Jesus through the Blessed Virgin Mary. I was sitting in my living room. This was perhaps the first time that I felt I truly understood the Total Consecration. It is the giving of yourself totally to Mary so that she might use your merits to more effectively and more perfectly bring about God's will in your life. Knowing God's will perfectly, Mary will apply your merits where they will best be used. The vehicle is Mary, but the object is Jesus.

I put down the consecration book and began pondering what should be done with Patrick. The previous night I had witnessed a ghostly pale, bony, unkempt, empty shell of a young man limp through my door. This was my son? His once-vibrant smile was downturned. His formerly sparkling eyes had a vacant stare. His arms showed scars and track marks. Seeing him this way made me feel as if I were looking death in the face. Had I failed as a father? How long could Patrick live in this condition? When would I receive that devastating phone call?

I reflected on all we had been through. Mindful of how St. Monica had prayed thirty years for her son, Augustine, my wife and I had been referring to Patrick as our St. Augustine. We hoped and prayed that, like St. Augustine, our son would turn from his worldly ways and turn back to God.

Nothing we had done for Patrick seemed to have helped him. Of course we prayed for him. His entire family prayed for him. Prayer never goes to waste. But by all outward appearances, the only change we saw in him was for the worse. Patrick had been in and out of numerous detox and rehabilitation programs, to no avail. He was still addicted and close to self-destruction. He had one foot in the grave and was a breath away from the possibility of hell.

I sat there, still pondering. My thoughts returned to the Mother of God. I earnestly prayed. "Mary, I have done everything I know how to do for Patrick. I don't know what else I can do to help him. I give him to you. Take him. He is yours." And that was that. I accepted myself as powerless and gave everything over to the Mother of Jesus.

It was only a week later that my mother-in-law mentioned a place named Cenacolo (Cha-nock-a-low). Our priest, Fr. Bob, had mentioned this place to her. He knew about Cenacolo because he had visited their community in Medjugorje, where the Mother of God is reported to have been appearing to six visionaries since 1981. Cenacolo has communities at other Marian sites such as Knock, Ireland, and Lourdes, France. It must have been providential, because Fr. Bob did not know about Patrick's condition. We proposed this new avenue of recovery to Patrick.

Yes, I cried to the Blessed Mother for help. And from Patrick's blog, apparently he was begging for help as well, though doubtful that the needed help would come.

Patrick blogged:
> My life is in shambles as my self-esteem takes another hit,
> My body is aching and my mind is full of @#$%,
> My veins are collapsing and my eyes are all bloodshot,
> I have no value left and a great big nothing is what I got,
> Another rehab is calling and I know just what they'll say,
> Don't do drugs sonny—that's the wrong way to play,

But could this one succeed and give me a way out,
Help me—help me is all I'm @#$%^&^& able to shout.
Cenacolo is a faith-based recovery community. They have centers in Florida and Alabama, and their program is free of charge. But acceptance is conditional on an interview process. It seemed that this would be too good to be true, that he would agree to go and then be accepted.

Praise the Lord! Patrick was accepted and agreed to stay. Within several weeks he was at Cenacolo located in St. Augustine, Florida, at Our Lady of Hope Farm. How providential! Our St. Augustine was at St. Augustine, Florida. And my Lady of Hope had placed him at the Our Lady of Hope Farm. Cenacolo is commonly referred to simply as, Community.

After his Cenacolo interview and before entering Community, he had to return home for two weeks. These were the most difficult two weeks in his life and in mine. The seduction of drugs was so strong that we couldn't let him out of our sight. One night we spent the entire time until morning driving from hospital to hospital attempting to get him admitted. He didn't trust himself to stay clean and was hoping to be drugged to sleep at the hospital. Though I knew that he didn't meet the criteria for being admitted, the night was useful to the extent that it got us through to another day without him using drugs. When he did sleep, we slept together. Patrick and I agreed to sleep with our wrists handcuffed together so that there was no way for him to slip out and shoot up with drugs.

When the devil sees that one is about to undertake a sublime and holy task, he does everything in his power to ruin things. And we were no exception. Despite our best efforts, Patrick was not under our control twenty-four hours a day. On the evening before his scheduled flight to Florida, we sent him out to the grocery store. He didn't return home for a long while. Upon his return, he was without the car that he had driven to the store. The story we got was this. He had gone to somebody's house. And at that house was a dealer who claimed that Patrick owed him money. The dealer produced a gun and demanded payment. Patrick had no money on him but promised that if let go, he would return with the money. The dealer agreed under two conditions. Patrick would have to leave his passport with the dealer and leave his keys to the car parked out back. Hence, Patrick walked home.

What a quandary! He would need the passport for his trip the next day. This was a requirement, because Cenacolo Community members are often sent overseas. Knowing this, I sprang into action, grabbed our spare car keys, and sprinted to that house in order to survey the situation. We didn't want to involve the police, because that might delay Patrick's departure.

The car was parked in the middle of a parking lot behind the house. No other cars were parked anywhere near the impounded car. To avoid detection, I got onto my belly and crawled across the parking lot. Reaching the car, I eased open the passenger door and stretched across the seat. Hunching as low as possible, I started the car and raced out of the parking lot.

With our car safely out of harm's way, the next task was to procure Patrick's passport. Summoning all of my courage, I returned to the house on foot and, with a trembling finger, rang the doorbell. With fervent prayers in my heart, mind, and soul, I waited with foreboding. A nondescript, benign-looking guy answered the door. I told him that I was Patrick's father, and I'd come for his passport and keys. The guy said, "Sure." He went to the coffee table, picked them up, and handed them to me. Praise God! The only sour note to the outcome of this event was the milk Patrick had left in the car. By this time, it was indeed sour.

With two weeks of difficulty behind us, we drove to the airport, and Patrick was off to Florida. What a burden was relieved when he finally arrived at Cenacolo's Our Lady of Hope Farm. This situation set Patrick upon his new destiny.

Anne remembers it well.
> But hope was reborn after we found the wonderful Community of Cenacolo and took Patrick to Florida. At first, I still couldn't let myself believe that this would be the answer. After years of the roller coaster, it was hard to truly trust. My emotions were spent and I had become a bit cynical and definitely unforgiving. The process of the spiritual healing was very gradual with lots of ups and downs for our entire family. But the end result of a change within my son would make everything I have been through totally worth it! If he could only become clean, healthy, and happy again!

Patrick's sister Sally again shares her perspective.
> Whenever Patrick embarked upon recovery, I was glad obviously, but also felt like our family was still all focused on Patrick, just for a different reason now. It was like wow, first he gets everyone's attention and focus for being bad, and now he gets it all for being good. But here I was being good all along and it seems that no one cares? I was only a teen at the time, so obviously my thinking was immature, but I remember being pretty mad the first time I saw him recovered. It was like really…he's clean now so all is forgiven? All those years of lying, stealing, and causing stress…and we are just supposed to forgive? Obviously I am over this now but it's definitely true that there is a whole lot of resentment attached to being the family member of an addict. It's always all about them, whether it's good or bad.

Two of Jesus's parables are at play with Sally and her siblings. The first is that of the Lost Sheep: "Which one of you, having a hundred sheep and losing one of them, does not leave the ninety-nine in the wilderness and go after the one that is lost until he finds it?" (Luke 15:4).

Sally is correct. At times, Anne and I were so distracted by Patrick's misdeeds that it became all encompassing. Our attention was often diverted away from our other children and focused on Patrick.

The other parable applicable here is that of the prodigal son. This parable is very familiar to many people. In this story we have a son who demands his inheritance from his father. Getting the money, the son leaves home and begins living a life of debauchery. When a famine hits, the son has no money left and decides to return to the father, offering profound apologies. The father, seeing his prodigal son returning from far off, commands his servants to kill the fatted calf for a feast celebrating the son's return.

> Now his elder son was in the field; and when he came and approached the house, he heard music and dancing. He called one of the slaves and asked what was going on. He replied, "Your brother has come, and your father has killed the fatted calf, because he has got him back safe and sound." Then he became angry and refused to go in. His father came out and began to plead with him. But he answered his father, "Listen! For all these years I have been working like a slave for you, and I have never disobeyed your command; yet you have never given me even a young goat so that I might celebrate with my friends. But when this son of yours came back, who has devoured your property with prostitutes, you killed the fatted calf for him!" Then the father said to him, "Son, you are always with me, and all that is mine is yours. But we had to celebrate and rejoice, because this brother of yours was

dead and has come to life; he was lost and has been found."
(Luke 15:25–32)

So yes, Sally's feelings are a quite common reaction to such a situation. She had lived according to her parents' wishes and had been obedient. Yet her brother, who had caused distress in the family, got both the negative and positive attention.

Let us now return to Patrick's new life at Cenacolo.

Patrick's life-changing experience:
Despite our diligence, Patrick had still managed to smuggle drugs into the Community grounds. We got a phone call about a week after his admittance, telling us that they had found a stash of his drugs, hidden away in a crook of the stone wall surrounding the compound. It was not until years later that we would learn just how tenuous was his commitment to stay there.

In the mornings, the men in Community gather for Eucharistic adoration in the chapel on their compound. But for the first two weeks, the new Community members are not permitted to join this morning prayer. Patrick schemed that this morning time when the other men were praying would be an excellent time for him to escape. He figured that he would live on the beach, find some drugs, and live his life in freedom. He was free to leave of his own volition at any time, but he realized that if the other men knew he intended to leave, they would be successful in talking him out of it.

His plan was put into play one evening about ten days after his arrival. He packed his clothes into a plastic garbage bag and threw them over the four-foot stone wall for easy access in the morning. He would awake early, jump the wall, and head for the St. Augustine beach.

In the morning, there was a deluge of a rainstorm. Standing in this rain for even ten seconds would have resulted in being totally drenched. So Patrick put off his escape until the next morning. Lo and behold, the next day there was another torrential storm just like the first. His plan delayed again, Patrick arose early on the third day and found the same condition. Once again he was forced to delay his departure. On the fourth day, there was another deluge! His plans were foiled again. But there was another plan afoot of which he was unaware. God had a definite plan for him.

On this fourteenth day in Community, he would finally be permitted to attend the morning Eucharistic adoration, so he was unable to make his escape at the planned time.

Catholics believe that the Eucharist is actually the Body of Christ, as Jesus spoke of in the discourse on the bread of life (John 6). This adoration is a solemn experience, undertaken with the utmost reverence and respect. After the Mass, Eucharistic adoration is the highest form of praise to God.

On that fourteenth morning, Patrick went to the chapel with his Community brothers. He was well acquainted with this form of Eucharistic prayer. We had done it many times as a family. But this time for Patrick, it was different. He entered the chapel. Many of the men were already kneeling on the wooden floor in front of the tabernacle, so he joined them.

Patrick looked upon the Eucharistic Host reposed in a golden monstrance. As he gazed, Patrick felt an intense love from God that he had never before felt. He could feel God's love being poured upon him. Love radiated from the Host and enflamed his heart. A pure and total agape love saturated Patrick's being. He could sense the immeasurable mercy of God. Patrick's heart began to burn with love for Christ. All of his former religious fervor returned to him, and more. At that moment, his life changed. He knew that God loved him and wanted him to stay in Community. He immediately turned away from drugs and immorality and returned to God. And he has never looked back. Patrick has returned to the light!

Since that date, over nine years ago, Patrick has become a new man. He completed his three years of the Cenacolo "school of life." He has abandoned drugs and has embraced God.

Cenacolo (Cenacle, Upper Room) has over sixty centers around the world. After his three years of recovery in Community, he then aided in the opening of a Community house in Alabama and became the head of that Community. He then volunteered to become a missionary at a Cenacolo mission in Argentina, caring for young children. This would be his way of paying back Cenacolo and God, for saving his mortal life and saving his eternal life.

Those in Community live lives of work and prayer. They have the Blessed Sacrament reposed in their dormitories, pray three rosaries per day, and arise at two in the morning once a week for a Eucharistic holy hour.

Some years ago, Patrick told us that if he was still in the mission field when he turned thirty, he would consider this to be his life's vocation. At this writing, Patrick is beyond thirty years old. Furthermore, he stated that if he was still a missionary by the time he turned forty, he would consider becoming a priest! Patrick commented to me, "If I became a priest, you'd do backflips." I retorted, "Patrick, I'm doing backflips right now over your life." I then promised him that if he did become a priest, I'd go to Confession to him. (And he wouldn't even have to pay me twenty dollars like I'd paid him in the past.)

If I were to write the itinerary for Patrick's life, I could not have even hoped for all that has been accomplished through the hands of the Blessed Mother. Thank you, most Blessed Mother. You are truly Our Mother of Hope. Thank you, Most Holy Trinity!

I attribute my surrender of Patrick to Mary, and his recovery directly to the Total Consecration. Patrick also had done the Consecration in his childhood. The Total Consecration to Jesus through Mary is an integral part of the Community's spirituality.

By making this Consecration to Mary, you are placing yourself completely and totally in her hands. You are giving her permission to form you, discipline you, and mold you into a true follower of Christ. Mary will only do God's will. So her guidance is perfect.

Background on Cenacolo:
>Comunità Cenacolo America is part of the international Comunità Cenacolo, Community of the Cenacolo, founded in Italy in 1983 by a religious sister named Elvira Petrozzi. Sister Elvira felt that God was calling her to serve the poor of the modern world: to serve disillusioned young men and women who live in desperation and hopelessness, convinced that life has no meaning or value. Unable to find peace or joy in their lives, they seek to fill the emptiness with the illusory pleasures of the world, only to find themselves steeped in an intense interior isolation. Trusting unwaveringly in the direction of the Holy Spirit, Sister Elvira proclaims to all those who live in darkness that only Jesus Christ can heal and transform their shattered lives, changing despair into hope, sadness into joy, hatred into forgiveness, and death into life.
>
>The Cenacolo is not so much a therapeutic community or drug rehab center as a school of life with prayer at its heart. The young people are thus put through a kind of intensive

spiritual boot camp where they learn to live in a totally new way—to accept a simple lifestyle and to rediscover the gifts of work, friendship and of faith in the Word of God, instead of relying on the crutch of drugs to escape from everything that is too painful to deal with. In their brochure the Cenacolo members explain their biggest problems are not the chemical withdrawals but reorienting their lives.

The program also teaches the addict to embrace the suffering and pain in their lives and give it to Christ through prayer, particularly in front of the Blessed Sacrament. Thus they learn in a practical way that these things can be carried with the grace of God and the love of community without having to resort to chemical escape mechanisms. Those who successfully complete the program emerge not just healed of their addiction but strong, vibrant Christians with a heart to give and serve, particularly to help others who are suffering in the way they did in the past.
(http://www.comunitacenacolo.org)

As mentioned earlier, in mid-2007 Patrick agreed to enter the Cenacolo Community. When Patrick first went to Florida to enter Cenacolo, it was about six months before we again saw him.

We went to a Festival of Life in St. Augustine. As we and many other parents waited to see our sons, we were ushered into a church where the Blessed Sacrament was exposed. Upon entering and kneeling down, we saw Patrick, along with other young men, kneeling in front of the altar in deep prayer. They rose and sang some religious songs, facing the tabernacle.

What a joy to see these former addicts praising God with such fervor! After the service, the young men went to their parents. I grabbed Patrick into a deep embrace, and neither of us let go for a long while. I felt like the father of the prodigal son. "For this son of mine was dead and is alive again; he was lost and is found." At that moment while I had my arms around Patrick in the chapel, I had seen the clarity in his eyes that had not been there for several years. I could sense the resurgence of faith in his soul. I could see the joy in his smile. I was holding on to my renewed son. He was dead, but now he is alive!

This prolonged time of embrace was the happiest moment of my life, and it remains so to this day.

In reflection, I kept thinking to myself, "How good God is, to bring these young men and women back from the death of sin, into the light of His love." This reflects Cenacolo's motto: "From Darkness to the Light." How great is His love and how complete His healing!

Anne had a similar experience when we attended a Festival of Life in Saluzzo, Italy.

> It had been a year since Patrick had entered Community. He was living in Italy and had encouraged us to attend this celebration of twenty-five years since Cenacolo's founding. Our trek getting there had been difficult. We'd lost luggage and had missed a flight. Everything was strange to me, for I had never been out of the United States.
>
> Here we were in this foreign country, amid a thousand people attending this Festival of Life. We didn't even know if we would be able to see Patrick. He had been living in another location, quite a distance from Saluzzo.
>
> As we scaled the formidable hillside leading to the Cenacolo mother house, I became quite winded. We scanned the crowd, looking for Patrick. How would we ever find him in this crowd?

Suddenly he appeared. Oblivious to the people around me, I shouted out with joy and exuberance, "There's my son!" I ran the twenty yards between us like I had never run before. I threw myself into his arms and basked in the joy of our reunion. All the worries of the past melted away when I saw the light and happiness in his eyes. He was radiant with health and joy! His words as we embraced were calm and loving. Our conversations came easily, and we got to talk about everything and forgive. We had a wonderful visit, filled with lots of laughing and hugging. I was so proud of him. My son was healed!

This journey of Cenacolo, however, is not solely for the person entering Community. It is intended to be a journey for the entire family. It is by advancing together in faith that true healing takes place. And hopefully, through this journey, we all learn to control our own addictions. Each of us has some sort of addiction. It could be the pursuit of money, power, or ego. It could be any number of worldly goals or pleasures. Cenacolo teaches that only by being centered on Christ can we be happy in life and in eternity. Here I reiterate the words of St. Augustine: "Our hearts are restless, Lord, and they will not rest until they rest in you." To achieve full healing for the addict and for the family, this spiritual journey needs to be a movement of the entire family.

Throughout the world today, drug addiction has become a scourge that has the potential to destroy our civilized society. Sociologists, psychologists, doctors, therapists, and other professionals have attempted to stem the tide of addicts flooding the clinics. While many people are helped in these facilities, a vast majority are not. One problem is that many clinics ignore a vital element in the solution to these behaviors. Alcoholics Anonymous and Narcotics Anonymous have indeed tapped into this answer, but they are an exception. Actually, Alcoholics Anonymous began as a Catholic-based recovery program. But they became more generically Christian for a broader appeal. I offer kudos to them for their God-centered approach.

But for the most part, for our society in general, the importance of God has been minimized and often ignored. It is this minimized factor that is actually the key to the very process of recovery. Reportedly, Cenacolo has a recovery rate of about 98 percent for those who complete the program. Mother Elvira has the problem of drug addiction analyzed and solved in one sentence. She firmly believes and has proven: "The solution to addiction is Jesus Christ."

God certainly works in strange ways. Everything He permits to happen to us can be brought to good. My son is an example. Had he always been an average Joe and never done drugs, he would probably still be that average Joe in most things, including his spirituality. But because he was exposed to the face of evil and experienced the depravity of the drug culture, he was able to soar above it. This mechanism works like pulling on a rubber band. A person can be pulled further and further from God. And when the tension is released, there is a quick and forceful return and momentum to experience God even closer than before. Had Patrick never done drugs, he would not have become a missionary, living and working with the Cenacolo nuns.

Patrick has even gone so far as to be thankful to God that he went through his addiction, because this is what finally brought him back to God. The religion that he had once thought was unnecessary is precisely what saved his life. His faith and his religion saved not only his mortal life but also his eternal life.

Because of his addiction, Patrick had experienced living with spiritual giants and has seen a multitude of miracles of Divine Providence. In Community, the members grow their own crops and raise animals for their food. But for everything else they need, they pray for it. The Community doesn't put out a request for the many items needed for day-to-day living. They pray for it—and what they need always comes. It is amazing how exacting God is in providing to them just what they need. A book could be written on the miracles of grace experienced at the Cenacolo Communities. Each person who enters Community and is healed is the greatest miracle. But in all matters, great or small, Divine Providence provides everything needed by Cenacolo, because they totally trust in God.

You must believe in miracles! I experienced a miracle in the life of my son. You too can have this happen to your loved one. Have *faith* in God. Have *hope* that the cure from addiction will come. Remember that *love* overcomes all. May our Lord bless and heal you and bring healing to your loved ones.

In the most condensed form, Patrick has at times shared how his life has changed. Apparently, this comment resonates with addicts, for it is something they never experience. Speaking directly to the mindset of an addict, Patrick says, "I go to bed happy."

In the writing of Patrick's story, I have redoubled my thanksgiving to God that Patrick is still alive. I thank God every time I see Patrick. I thank God every time I think of Patrick. I ponder, "How good God is. Praised be His holy name!"

Anne reflects:
> My heart bursts with pride at my son's progress and growth! He is an amazing man—full of love. He cares about God and cares for others more than about himself. I could not have asked for a better outcome.
>
> I can honestly say now in retrospect that the hard times we went though were totally worth it. My son's path was rocky

and full of twists and turns for us all, but God pulled everything together for the good.

Throughout this ordeal, Patrick put his body through torture and his life at mortal risk nearly every day of his senior-high-school years and after. He dragged his soul through the depths of sin and depravity. It is truly a miracle that he came through all of this with his life intact. And by the grace of God, his soul has also recovered from the wanton misuse of his free will. Without knowing the story, and looking at Patrick's history of drug abuse through an unbiased eye, one could be certain that this person would have died of an overdose. Praise God for His protection of Patrick!

I think of all of the teenagers and young adults I know of who have died from drug overdose. It breaks my heart to see this happen. And I wonder why Patrick's life was spared. He is the one who took things to the max. He is the one who constantly pushed the envelope. He is the one who had no restraints, always attempting to get higher and higher. Somehow, his reckless actions did not result in his imprisonment, overdose, or death—though they did leave him with the legacy of hepatitis C.

I have great empathy when attempting to console people who have lost the life of their child to drugs. At times this becomes uncomfortable; I wonder if they are thinking about how they lost their child, yet mine was saved. It is such a great tragedy to lose someone in such a way. It is senseless. So much talent and so many good people have fallen victim to drug addiction and have paid with their lives. Often these deaths fracture the families involved as blame is assigned or faith in God is shaken. This scourge of drug abuse must be stopped.

Patrick's recovery is a testament to what is, in my estimation, the best route to recovery. His walk gave recovery not only to his body but also to his soul. His journey has been a journey of returning to God. He has traveled from the darkness into the light.

And Sr. Elvira is so correct in her assessment: *"The solution to addiction is Jesus Christ."*

Patrick's story continues in the following chapters and concludes after "Patrick's Words." But first, let us now look at some concrete spiritual steps that can be taken with and for the addict.

Prayer Strategies

In rescuing a person in the throes of addiction, prayer is necessary. This prayer is obviously needed by the addict. The more people there are praying for the addict, the better the chances of recovery. However, God has still given this addict a free will. Despite prayers, this person may choose to ignore and fight against the helps that God will send. The goal is to have the person give up taking illegal drugs and, from a Christian perspective, have him or her also turn to God.

Sometimes the impetus needed will not come until the time of death. A final penitence may be the grace received. If this happens, that is enough, because it means for the person an eternity in Heaven.

Dismas, the Good Thief, who hung on the cross beside Jesus, had this final penitence. In fact, we know for sure that Dismas is in Heaven. Jesus said to him, "Today you will be with Me in Paradise." Now, this crucified former thief is known as Saint Dismas.

It might very well be that your prayers are the force needed to turn your loved one from drugs and all of the vices that this life entails. One must never give up hope. Prayers will aid the addict, but it is up to the addict to respond to God's call.

Additionally, prayers are needed for the family of the addict. While you are praying for the addict, prayers are needed not only by you but also for you. Prayers from others will give you strength. Knowing that people are praying for you will give you hope. And the fact that you yourself are praying will not only have an effect on the addict, but it will also affect the person offering those prayers. Even if the addict does not change, you will have changed.

Those who have lost hope when a tragedy has befallen them often ask: Why pray? St. Augustine (AD 354–430) has the answer to this question.

Why in our fear of not praying as we should, do we turn to so many things, to find what we should pray for? Why do we not say instead, in the words of the psalm: *I have asked one thing from the Lord, this is what I will seek: to dwell in the Lord's house all the days of my life, to see the graciousness of the Lord, and to visit his temple?* There, the days do not come and go in succession, and the beginning of one day does not mean the end of another; all days are one, simultaneously and without end, and the life lived out in these days has itself no end.

So that we might obtain this life of happiness, he who is true life itself taught us to pray, not in many words as though speaking longer could gain us a hearing. After all, we pray to one who, as the Lord himself tells us, knows what we need before we ask for it.

Why He should ask us to pray, when he knows what we need before we ask him, may perplex us if we do not realize that our Lord and God does not want to know what we want (for he cannot fail to know it), but wants us rather to exercise our desire through our prayers, so that we may be able to receive what he is preparing to give us. His gift is very great indeed, but our capacity is too small and limited to receive it. That is why we are told: Enlarge your desires, do not bear the yoke with unbelievers.

The deeper our faith, the stronger our hope, the greater our desire, the larger will be our capacity to receive that gift, which is very great indeed. *No eye has seen it;* it has no color. *No ear has heard it;* it has no sound. *It has not entered man's heart;* man's heart must enter into it.

> In this faith, hope and love we pray always with unwearied desire. However, at set times and seasons we also pray to God in words, so that by these signs we may instruct ourselves and mark the progress we have made in our desire, and spur ourselves on to deepen it. The more fervent the desire, the more worthy will be its fruit. When the Apostle tells us: *Pray without ceasing (I Thes. 5:16),* he means this: Desire unceasingly that life of happiness which is nothing if not eternal, and ask it of him who alone is able to give it. (Augustine's letter [130] on prayer)

St. Augustine did not always act in a saintly manner. In his own words, he described himself as a serious sinner. In fact, for much of his early life, he was a man of the world. He was a partier; he loved the female of the species and was prolific in his pursuit of their affections. These pursuits resulted in Augustine having a child out of wedlock. His mother, Monica, prayed unceasingly for Augustine. She continually pursued him with a plea that he turn from his sinful ways and turn to God.

Monica herself once suffered addiction to alcohol. It was her servant who pointed this out to her. Monica took this observation to heart and put away her drinking binges. But it took some time before Monica was able to persuade her husband to follow suit. Eventually he too gave up the drink. However, there was still the matter of their son, Augustine.

In 383, Augustine moved to Milan. He had hoped that this move from Hippo, in Africa to Italy would free him of his mother's holy badgering. But his mother followed him there. She was relentless. While in Milan, he was heavily influenced by the bishop who would become St. Ambrose. His sermons removed Augustine's intellectual objections to Christianity. Eventually Augustine was able to pray, "Make me chaste, (Lord) but not yet." He enjoyed his sinfulness too much to give it up just yet. At one point, however, Augustine was persuaded to read *The Life of Anthony*.

> I opened it and read silently the first paragraph that my eyes fell upon: "Not in orgies or drunkenness, not in promiscuity and licentiousness, not in rivalry and jealousy. But put on the Lord Jesus Christ, and make no provision for the desires of the flesh" (Rom. 13:13–14 NAB). I did not need to read any further. Instantly as the sentence ended, all my gloomy doubt vanished, dispelled by a saving light infused into my heart. (Augustine)

(Patrick's infusion of God's grace was much like that of Augustine).

Augustine's conversion was complete. It took thirty years of prayer before Monica's pleas for her son were answered. Augustine went on to become a priest and a bishop, and posthumously, he was named a doctor of the Catholic Church. Augustine led the North African church of Hippo for four decades, and he built many monastic communities. Upon his death, Augustine received the honor of being canonized a saint. Today we know this mother and son as St. Monica and St. Augustine.

Can you become a Monica for your loved one who is consumed by worldly desires much like Augustine? Monica never gave up on her son; she prayed without ceasing. And she remained close to him. Let us now ask St. Monica to pray for us and intercede for us.

Saint Monica Prayer
Dear Saint Monica, you were once the mournful mother of a prodigal son. Your faithfulness to prayer brought you and your son so close to God that you are now with him in eternity. By your intercession and God's grace, your son, St. Augustine, became a great and venerable saint of the church.

Please take my request to God with the same fervor and persistence with which you prayed for your own son. (Mention your intentions here.)

With your needs, worries, and anxieties, you threw yourself on the mercy and providence of God. Through sorrow and pain, you constantly devoted yourself to God. Pray for me, that I might join you in such a deep faith in God's goodness and mercy. Above all, dear Saint Monica, pray for me that I may, like your son, turn from my sin and become a great saint for the glory of God. Amen.

The above example surely illustrates the need for constant prayer. And Monica's example shows true perseverance. In the following pages, I wish to offer you some prayer strategies that have been proven to work. Remember, however, that answers to prayers are dispensed upon the desire of God. We cannot order God to bring about a certain result. God's ways are not our ways, and we cannot always see the wisdom in what He allows to happen.

And know that holy medals and other sacramentals are not good-luck charms. It is our faith expressed in our prayers and actions that can bring about answers to prayer. We express faith in our pleas to God. We express hope in our desired outcome and by trusting in God's Divine Providence. And we express love. Our prayers and actions express a love of God and love for our addict. The sacramentals are simply reminders and vehicles in helping us express this Faith, Hope and Love.

Jesus often told those whom he healed, "Your faith has healed you" (Mark 10:52). Work to increase your faith through prayer and good works. Strive for holiness. It is this pursuit of holiness that may unlock the floodgates of God's blessings upon you and upon your loved ones. Keep in mind Saint Augustine's words: "The deeper our

faith, the stronger our hope, the greater our desire, the larger will be our capacity to receive that gift, which is very great indeed."
Below, I have included some proven methods to help ourselves and others overcome sin and addiction. Seven proven methods are as follows: pray deeply and ask for the prayers of others, the rosary, the rosary preparation prayer, thirty-three-day preparation for Total Consecration, fifty-four-day rosary novena, the Hedge of Thorns, and the green scapular.

Our prayers are only as powerful as our faith. Strive to make yourself holy and offer everything through Mary that she might make your prayers perfect for Jesus. We say, "Hail Mary"; she says, "Hail Jesus."

Prayer
Your personal prayers will bring you closer to God and reap abundant blessings upon those for whom you pray. Seek out holy people and ask for their prayers as well. Prayer is the key. Prayer is essential!

The Rosary
The rosary is often a point of departure between Catholics and non-Catholics. Many believe that Catholics worship the Virgin Mary through this prayer. However, nothing could be further from the truth. Mary is only the means; Christ is the object. Meditating on the mysteries of the rosary is simply meditating on the life of Jesus, through the eyes of Mary. And the words of the Hail Mary prayer simply repeat scripture. Mary, the Mother of Jesus, is the Mother of us all. It is heartening to see that more and more non-Catholics are turning to the rosary as a means to grow closer to God. In the Gospel, upon being greeted by her cousin Elizabeth, Mary proclaims, "All generations shall call me blessed." And this Catholics do.

After the Mass and Eucharistic Adoration, many Catholics consider the rosary to be next in the hierarchy of effective prayers. Countless miracles throughout history have been attributed to the rosary. In modern times, the bloodless revolution in the Philippines is attributed directly to the rosary. Cardinal Sin of Manila called the people into the streets to pray the rosary and march on the Marcos palace. The palace guards had orders to shoot to kill. But the praying marchers walked right past the guards, and not a shot was fired. The dictator Marcos was then deposed. Later, the general of the palace guards testified that as the villagers approached the palace, he saw a woman descend from the sky. She held up her hands in a gesture telling him not to harm the people. She said, "Do not harm my children." He believed that this woman was the Blessed Mother of Jesus. Pray the rosary. It is a most powerful prayer.

The Rosary Preparation Prayer
I heard a priest speak at my parish. He was an associate of Fr. Gino, who was an associate of St. Padre Pio, the stigmatic, who bore the five wounds of Jesus. This priest came to my parish and said that if you want to save your family, say this prayer prior to praying your rosary: "Through this rosary, I bind my family to the Sacred Heart of Jesus and the Immaculate Heart of Mary." This I do before my daily rosary.

Thirty-Three-Day Preparation for Total Consecration, by St. Louis de Montfort
Pope John Paul II said that this consecration changed his entire spirituality. He lived this consecration every day and recited the consecration every day. He had as his papal motto *"Totus Tuus"* (Totally Yours, to Jesus through Mary). This is the consecration I did when I gave Patrick to Mary, and within a couple of weeks, he was at Cenacolo. This is a most wonderful act of consecration that many misunderstand at first, but it becomes a lifeblood if done

faithfully. A more modern version of this Consecration is called, Thirty-three Days to Morning Glory.

The Fifty-Four-Day Rosary Novena
This is the prayer prayed by my wife's grandparents for their daughter who was born with cerebral palsy. She had been having nightly seizures from birth to about one year old. On the last night of the novena, the baby slept throughout the night and had no more seizures. We also prayed this novena for a person in addiction treatment and in marital trouble. We were in the process of doing this novena when Patrick went to Cenacolo. Everything was resolved in a wonderful way and remains that way today. See http://www.medjugorje.com/download/booklets/288-54+Day+Rosary+Novena.html for more information.

Hedge of Thorns
This focused and intentional prayer should be used when someone we love needs a specific protection by letting God erect a wall of spiritual protection. We call it the building of a spiritual hedge of thorns that will keep the enemy's forces out. Psalms 24:3–4 (Living) states, "Who may stand before the Lord? Only those with pure hands and hearts, who do not practice dishonesty and lying." There are several major prerequisites for this prayer to be effective.

You must have a clear conscience and pure motivation. This means that there is no unconfessed sin in your life and that your motivation for this prayer is for the well-being of another. If you are holding on to unresolved sin or resentment toward anyone, confess it. God tells us in his Word, "*If we confess our sins,* He is faithful and just and will forgive us our sins and purify us from all unrighteousness" (1 John 1:9). Once this hedge is placed on somebody, assuming all conditions are met, it will not be removed until consciously removed by the person who prayed it in place. It may happen that it will bring troubles that cause the person to come back to God—whatever it takes will happen.

Hedge of Thorns Prayer

I bind you, satan, and come against your power in the name and blood of the Lord Jesus Christ. I am armed with the blood and the word of God (*my sword*). Right now I pierce you through with the truth that Jesus Christ came in the flesh to destroy your works.

Even now as I lift my praises to God the Father, the *powers* and *principalities* over my home are bound with fetters of iron and chains of the blood of Jesus Christ. Whatever I bind on Earth is bound in Heaven, and with that authority I cast you down. I let loose the victory and power of the Lord Jesus Christ on my home.

By faith, I scatter every evil force arrayed against my home, as holy angels smite them in my behalf. Greater is He that is with us, and more powerful are those with us than with you. The Father Himself sent His Word to deliver us from your devices.

I put to flight every demonic power that would harm my family and bind all spiritual activity in [name]. I claim victory for [name] through the shed blood of the Lord Jesus Christ. I let loose the power of the Holy Spirit in [name]'s life and bind all workings of satan. I break his hold and spoil his goods in the authority and blood of the Lord Jesus Christ. You, satan and every one of your demonic angels are bound and defeated.

I especially bind and bring down to the judgment written every force that would hinder the working of the Holy Spirit in the life of [name]. I rejoice in the knowledge that you must bow before the name and blood of the Lord Jesus Christ.

By faith, I let loose the peace and power of God the Father, the grace of the Lord Christ on [name]. Holy Spirit, come and work with [name] for the glory of the Father through the Lord Jesus Christ. Father, pour out your agape love on [name].

Heavenly Father, I ask you, in the name and through the blood of the Lord Jesus Christ, to rebuke satan for taking captive that which you created and build a "hedge of thorns" around [name].

I pray that by this hedge the influence of all spiritual powers of satan will be defeated and [name] will be protected from spiritual attack. I bind satan and bring all the thoughts in the mind of [name] into captivity and the obedience of the Lord Jesus Christ. I pray that you seal this mind with the blood of the Lord Jesus Christ. Amen.

Thank You, Lord; I believe it is done.

The answer to addiction is multifaceted but is also quite simple. *Everything* hinges on prayer. Through your personal holiness, tremendous graces can be granted to your loved one who has been captured by drugs and ensnared by the devil. Our only hope is in the Lord, who made Heaven and Earth. Give your life to God. Let every breath you take give praise to Him. Let every beat of your heart be for the Lord. In this spiritual state, your life will be ripe for God to bring about miracles for you.

History is full of stories of divine intervention in human affairs. God loves us. He loves our addicted loved ones. God loves that addict more than it is possible for any human to love. But God relies on us to be channels of His grace. Open your mind to God's Word. Open your heart to God's love. Open your daily actions to His promptings. Once you do everything for God, miraculous things will happen.

And I urge you; have recourse to the Blessed Mother. She will lead you to Jesus. Jesus's first miracle of *grace* came through Mary in His Incarnation. He was born of Mary's womb. Jesus's first miracle of *nature* also came through Mary as she prompted him to help the newly married couple who had run out of wine. And the blessings of Jesus continue to come through Mary.

She will speak for us as she spoke for the married couple at Cana. And her instruction to the servants at Cana is the same as her instruction to us. Even as Jesus told his Mother, "My time has not come," Mary told the servants, and indeed tells us, "Do whatever Jesus tells you." Though Jesus said that His time had not yet come, at His Mother's prompting, Jesus turned the wedding water into the finest wine.

The Green Scapular
This is the scapular that is given out by the Legion of Mary. It is the only scapular (I believe) that does not need to be worn to have its effect. I placed one under Patrick's mattress, and he became a missionary. If you could get it close to your loved one, in his or her car, home, or backpack, under the mattress, and so on, it might bring about good results. Remember, it is not superstition but the faith that accompanies this sacramental.

Remember, everything that ails us has recourse in prayer. Prayer brings about an intimacy with God. He draws close to us through prayer. No prayer ever goes unanswered. And the more we pray, the better we know for what we should pray. Pray without ceasing! Pray, pray, pray.

Practical Helps

The reasons leading to illegal drug use are numerous. The ways out of addiction are numerous also. For some, it simply takes a taste of reality, seeing what drugs have done to their life. For others, it takes a tragedy. Many have to hit rock bottom for them to wake up. For still others, it takes a miracle. Without a doubt, my son experienced a miracle. It was a true miracle. He went from the druggie who wouldn't deny a dare, to a missionary who does nothing but care.

Helping an addict to recovery is an arduous task. One gets the feeling that one is walking a tightrope. The parent wants to help his or her loved one, yet it is important not to enable the loved one. The line between helping and enabling is often not at all clear. My children thought that I enabled Patrick by paying many of his debts to keep him out of jail. I feel that I helped him by keeping him from sinking deeper into trouble, because he was still in high school. One thing is certain, however. Don't ever give money directly to the addict. We tried many tactics, but mostly we prayed. What we did for him, whether it was enabling or not—it worked. But none of it would have been successful without the Divine Providence of God.

It is amazing how God works. He can bring good out of anything and everything, if we let Him. Take, for instance, the biblical story of David and Bathsheba. King David's sins grew in seriousness as he continued to engage in them. Concerning Bathsheba, his first sin was that of lust. He saw her from his castle as she was taking a bath. He lusted. Wanting her, he summoned her to his palace. He then committed the sin of adultery. When she became pregnant, David schemed to make it seem as if the baby belonged to Bathsheba's husband, Uriah. David brought him back from battle and instructed him to go home. But sympathizing with his troops still in battle, he refused to enter his house and take pleasure in his wife. Realizing that he was being foiled, David gave orders to his general for Uriah to be put forward in battle, and to have his comrades withdraw, leaving Uriah to certain death. This was done, and Uriah was slaughtered.

How could any good possibly come from this string of David's offences against God? Eventually King David repented of his sins. He wore sack cloth and sat in ashes as a sign of his repentance. And God blessed him. Amazingly, the lineage of David and Bathsheba leads to Mary, Joseph, and Jesus, all of whom are of the House of David.

So it is with God. He brings good out of evil. Patrick is certainly a testament to God's transforming graces. This beat-down druggie, who pushed the envelope at every turn, who rejected religion, has returned to Christ religiously. And he has served Him by caring for the poor and needy orphans of Argentina. There will be more on this aspect of Patrick's life in a bit.

God has also used Patrick's addiction for good in my life. I've had countless opportunities to share his miraculous story with others. People have been inspired, and addicts have been spurred to seek recovery. In my ministry at the local prison, over half of the inmates attending the sessions are in jail for drug use. When I give them advice, they are usually in complete agreement with me on what needs to be done. They can sense that I know what I am talking about.

Because of Patrick, I have credibility with them. I've heard the men lament the clinical advice they've gotten from counselors, psychologists, and psychiatrists. I don't want to discredit these professionals. Many people are helped by them. But unless these professionals have been in the trenches and have seen and experienced firsthand the ins and outs, the ups and downs of the addict's life, they might not be able to understand the viewpoint of the addict. I've been blessed in that the path of Patrick's life has perfectly prepared me for this prison ministry. God is bringing good out of that horrible nightmare of Patrick's addiction.

The prisoners with whom I've spoken are almost unanimous in the belief that their imprisonment is a blessing. Out in the world, they had many distractions and obligations to keep them busy. But in jail, there is ample time. There is time to pray. There is time to reflect. There is time to heal. There is time to make peace with God. And there is time for a spiritual renewal.

You see, I've experienced the effects of addiction through my son. I lived with an addict. And through Patrick, as well as through Cenacolo, I've learned the mind of the addict. Much has been learned through the tempest of addiction. Let me share with you a portion of what I have learned.

Some of the advice I've given to the addicted prisoners is as follows:

Get in touch with God. Proper recovery takes more power than we as mere mortals possess. The addict needs to reach out for the infinite grace of God. We must rely on His mercy. Addiction recovery is a spiritual battle. To attempt this without using spiritual tactics is to deny the most essential means available. Read the Bible. Not only will this reading help in understanding God, but it will also build up a relationship with Him. And the very act of reading the Bible will shower blessings on the reader.

During drug use, the addict's flesh is ruling the spirit. Availing the self to God's help will make it easier for the spirit to rule the flesh. The devil is certainly employing every evil spiritual tactic at his disposal against the addict. By weakening the flesh through drug use, he weakens the will. An addicted person is fodder for the evil one. Many addicts will do *anything* to get their fix. And this necessitates committing sins and crimes to finance the feeding of their habit. The one and only focus in the life of an addict is to find the next fix. They need instead to become fixated on God, for He is the Divine Healer. AA and NA certainly realize the addict's need for God. Getting in touch with a higher power is the central theme of their recovery programs.

Don't think that you can only use "just a little bit." Once users are clean, often accomplished by time spent in jail, some think that they will just use a little but not return to the state of addiction previously experienced. This thinking is a fallacy. Initially, a new drug user builds up slowly to heavier use. It might take years to go from marijuana to heroin. But after getting clean and intending to cease the use of harder drugs, if they return to the marijuana, within weeks they will be back to their worst condition of using. And there is a good chance that they will go even further than before. In fact, a person with an addictive predisposition should not even be consuming alcohol. Marijuana is certainly the gateway drug to harder drugs, and alcohol will weaken the will, greatly increasing the probability of further drug abuse.

Make a drastic change in your life. The recovering addict must make drastic changes. One such vital change is a change in residence. Once clean addicts return to familiar surroundings, such as their hometown where they had always used, they invariably come across triggers. These triggers might be activated by the recovering addicts seeing places where they once got high or meeting people with whom they previously got high. It can be as simple as seeing a person with whom they've used. These experiences grasp ahold and seriously weaken the resolve to stay clean. Therefore, people attempting recovery need a new environment, and they need new friends. I've spoken with several inmates who had made a firm resolve to get clean, and they succeeded. But because they still hung around with the same old crowd, they got inadvertently implicated in an arrest and ended up back in jail. They definitely need new friends. Indeed, a recovering addict needs a new life.

All sin begins in the mind. We must first conceive of sin in our minds before it is expressed in actions. A temptation arises; we entertain it, dwell on it, and then start making plans to carry it out. And finally, the deed is done. The consequences of that sin are multifaceted, affecting the self and others. The best and easiest time to avoid sin is when it first enters the mind. The longer the thought remains, the harder it is to turn back. And as the thoughts turn to actions, it gets even more difficult to reconsider. This is why it is so important for a recovering addict to remain busy, filling the mind with purpose.

Once an addict, always an addict. This might seem to be a harsh assessment. However, people who have been addicted to drugs can never let their guard down. The addictive personality harbors a predisposition to abuse drugs, alcohol, or any other worldly offering. The difference lies in the question as to whether a person is an active addict or a clean addict (former user). The predisposition never disappears. But once people have obtained the will power and have gained control of their body, they can remain clean. Unfortunately, the addict is always in danger of relapsing. Constant care must be given for the addict to avoid occasions of temptation.

Join a church community. Part of the drastic change needed for recovery is gaining the support of a church community. An isolated addict is a hopeless addict. And a hopeless addict soon returns to being an active user. Those struggling with recovery (they all struggle) need to be kept busy. As the saying goes, "Idle hands are the devil's work." One of the strategies of AA is for a newly reformed user to attend thirty meetings in thirty days. Some AA groups advocate ninety meetings in ninety days. This constant reinforcement and peer support can get someone through those crucial first weeks or months of recovery. Add to this a vibrant and loving church community, and the recovering addict has a fighting chance. Addicts need someone whom they can trust, someone who believes in them. Unfortunately, at times, even churchgoers shy away from these very people who so need their help. There is strength in community. And there is holiness in seeking His Kingdom.

Look inward and look outward. Look inward at the beautiful soul God has provided to each of us. Spend time in silent prayer. Blessed Mother Teresa of Calcutta knew the value of silence. She had a saying: "The fruit of silence is prayer. The fruit of prayer is faith. The fruit of faith is love. The fruit of love is service. The fruit of service is peace." The addict is looking for peace. The peace of Christ is a great gift indeed. But it doesn't always come quickly or easily. Look inward, and see the wonderful creation of yourself that was put on Earth for a specific task. God has a mission for each of us. This mission is unique. Only you can fulfill your mission. Look inward and discover God's purpose for your life.

Look outward. Get involved in helping others. This might entail attending NA or AA meetings and being a sponsor. It might involve community service. It could be working with your church by witnessing your story or by evangelizing. People are in need everywhere. Find them and help them.

Keep busy. Get a job. Join a church, join AA or NA, or join a club. Get rid of bad thoughts. A scientist, in attempting to evacuate bad air from a beaker, can hook up a rubber stopper, insert a vacuum tube, and pump the air out of the beaker. This is a difficult task, and it is prone to leaks. But there is a much simpler way to eliminate air from that beaker. Just fill the beaker with water. So to eliminate the thoughts of using drugs, the thoughts of loneliness, the thoughts of the past, simply fill your mind with something else. Looking outward to the needs of others will go far in keeping bad thoughts away. And inviting God into your life will fill your mind with holy thoughts.

Love your neighbor and everyone. Love is the great healer. At the Final Judgment, love will cover a multitude of sins. Once a person gives love away, it is self-perpetuating. Every person seeks love. And the only way to gain love is to give it away. God is love. Love is God. All love comes from God. In loving God more, one's love of humankind naturally increases.

Addiction is the antithesis of love. Addiction involves a morbid self-love, which is not love at all. This self-love of the addict is expressed in constantly pleasing the body with high after high. But the reality is this. That self-love soon turns into self-loathing. The once-dreamy high turns into a never-ending nightmare. Love is the great escape. Love of God is the great beginning and the greatest ending.

We were created with a piece missing. There is a hole in our heart. Humans yearn to have this hole filled. We try to fill this hole with money. But money does not do the job. Therefore, we try to fill it with more money. If I've made $10 million, I'll try to make it $20 million. Or a person can try to fill that hole with power. Exerting power over family members, an employee, or anyone is an attempt to fill that void. You've heard the saying, "Power tends to corrupt. But absolute power corrupts absolutely." So power is not the answer. Some attempt to fill that void with worldly or bodily pleasures. Drug addicts fall into this category. Some use possessions. I already have a good, working Chevy. But I think I need a Maserati. That's OK for a while, until I set my eyes on a Ferrari. Try as we might, none of these things can satisfy that fundamental desire for something that will fill that void. We can find pleasure in these things. We can find comfort. But we won't find true happiness or joy.

If people only knew the secret, they would find the fulfillment that they so ardently desire. This fulfillment, the filling of the hole in our heart, can only be filled by God. Without God, there is no true happiness. Without God, there is no contentment. Without God, there is no love.

What about parents? What should parents do to prevent their children from experimenting with drugs or help them recover from addiction? Well, that's the million-dollar question, isn't it? While there is no guarantee or magic formula, there is a lot that parents can do.

As mentioned numerous times, do not give up hope. Even though addicts may have given up hope on themselves, they may be depending on your hope to sustain them. While in Argentina, Patrick wrote a poem for me. In it he chronicled our lives together, mentioning the special things that we had shared. One line of the poem really spoke to me. He wrote:

> I've had my ups and my downs, as in my life you can clearly see. I tell you this father, thank you much for never giving up on me.

Believe it or not, kids look up to their parents and want to please them. The extent to which this is true surprised me with Patrick. After his stint at Cedar Point, he moved to another state with Rachael. She was in college, and he gained employment at a local hospital.

When I would share this information with others, I knew that it was almost a given that they were assuming that Rachael and Patrick were living together. But they weren't. So I made it a point to mention that they had separate apartments. With so many couples cohabitating, I was proud of the fact that Patrick and Rachael were not living together. When we went to visit Patrick, we stayed at his place and frequently visited at Rachael's apartment.

It was not until years later that I learned the truth. Patrick and Rachael had indeed been living together. But Patrick had rented an apartment for the sole purpose of not disappointing his father. This was so important to him—me believing that they were living apart—that Patrick paid rent every month on an apartment that he never used.

Research shows that the main reason that kids don't use alcohol, tobacco, or drugs is because of their parents' positive influence. Kids don't want to disappoint their parents. That's why it is so important for parents to build a loving relationship with their kids and talk to them about substance abuse. Early and ongoing communication is essential in conveying proper values to the next generation.

A 2001 survey reported that one in five twelve- to seventeen-year-olds had used marijuana. About half of those who smoked cigarettes in the past month had also used illegal drugs. According to another study the same year, only one in twenty teens who did not smoke cigarettes or drink alcohol had used illegal drugs. Don't wait for things to get out of control. Let your kids know of your expectations for them. As the old adage goes, an ounce of prevention is worth a pound of cure.

At the outset, it is important to recognize who is most at risk of drug abuse. People with introverted personalities and who have fewer positive feelings are more likely to abuse drugs. Extroverted people who have more positive emotions are less likely to abuse drugs.

Statistics show that in situations of broken families, such as the lack of a male figure in the home, there is an increased likelihood of adolescent drug use and arrest. But the child in this situation entering the drug culture is definitely not a given. Fr. Patrick Peyton had a saying, "The family that prays together, stays together." This applies to all families, traditional and nontraditional. Family prayer is the strongest preventative medicine for potential victims of drug abuse.

A personality trait linked with substance abuse is one of negative emotionality or the tendency to experience negative feelings such as anxiety and depression. Low self-esteem can cause one to be inclined to use drugs. People who are very sensitive to punishment find, in drugs, something that allows them to escape. The sensitive child seems to have a susceptibility to drug abuse. The child who is easily hurt, and especially the ones who do not verbalize their hurt feelings, often turn to drugs for solace. That was the case with Patrick. Though he put on a tough persona, he could easily become slighted by an unkind word or by a person's doubt about his sincerity, or some such thing.

The openly defiant, antiestablishment rebel without a cause is certainly at risk. Which came first, the chicken or the egg? This is often the case with the rebels among us. Did their outlook lead them to drugs, or did drugs form their outlook? Another risk factor is low levels of a trait known as constraint—people who have compulsive behaviors, like the inability to stop a behavior or action once started, are susceptible to drug abuse.

Grandiosity is another—people who think that the world revolves around them may use drugs as a way of hiding their insecurity. People may be born with fewer dopamine receptors than others, but even legal drug use can also lower their numbers, possibly affecting personality and making people less extroverted, as well as increasing the risk for drug abuse. Listen to them all in a nonjudgmental way.

People who are antisocial may turn to drugs or alcohol to replace being social with other people. Lonely children may seek comfort or peer acceptance by becoming involved in drugs. Keep your finger on their pulse. Stay close. Young people are not as likely to get involved with drugs when caring adults are a part of their life. Talk *with* your children rather than talking *to* your children. Listen to them. Ask questions of them that can't be answered with a simple yes or no. Make it a priority to have meals together. Have family discussions.

Parents should never ever think that their child could not possibly be on drugs. Drugs are everywhere, and they affect every stratum of social and economic status. Nobody is immune. It is important to keep one's eyes open to look for signs. To deny the possibility that your child could be doing drugs is a foolish assumption.

Any sudden change in behavior, mood, appearance, appetite, or sleep patterns may be physical signs of drug use. Declining grades, missing money, a change in friends, air freshener or incense in their bedroom, and missing medicine may all indicate the behavioral changes that come with drug abuse. Psychological indicators may include irritability, angry outbursts, or laughing at nothing. Lack of motivation, the inability to focus, and a lethargic or spaced-out appearance may be indicators. If your child suddenly appears fearful, withdrawn, anxious, or paranoid with no apparent reason, it may indeed be caused by drug abuse. Any of the above items could have other causes. It is the parent's responsibility to investigate.

Don't be afraid to snoop. It is the parents' duty to keep their child safe. Sometimes this involves being the bad guy. Good parents cannot always be best buddies to their children. At times being a good parent involves invading their private space. A quick look through their dresser drawers and even under the mattress can reveal much. Computer tracking programs are a good tool for parents to keep tabs on their child. Of course, it is necessary that the child not know about that tracking program.

Finding the following items definitely points to drug use. Burned spoons are the result of melting drugs. Little green seeds found in pockets or drawers are usually marijuana. Pipes made of tin foil indicate that a drug has been inhaled. Plastic baggies are used to hold marijuana and cocaine. White powder is a strong indicator of drug use. Empty pen sections are used for snorting. Razorblades are employed to cut apart certain drugs. Hemostats, syringes, alligator clips, water pipes, and loose pills are all indicative of drug use. Small "stamp bags" contain heroin. The unexplained appearance of small rubber bands might indicate the use of these stamp bags. Rubber bands are often used in packaging them. Finding any of these items in the home should invoke a frank discussion with your child. If drugs are found, intervention of some sort is a must—immediately.

Intervention at the early stage may just involve having a discussion. The talk should be calm and compassionate without being judgmental. If the addiction has clearly manifested itself, you must be prepared. Have other loving family members present. Look for correct timing. Leave ample time for discussion. Be very careful in what you say and how you say it. You should express your expectations and consequences for the user. Have a possible plan ready. Have the phone number or web address of several rehabilitation clinics. Let your child choose which clinic he or she would be willing to attend. But be careful. Don't back yourself into a corner. Denials are sure to come. Expect to be rebuffed. Don't count on an immediate response. Recovery doesn't happen in a straight line. It can zigzag, and there are often relapses.

As is obvious, I am a strong supporter of family prayer. This creates a solid basis on which to build your family life. This promotes mutual love and respect. And it imparts wisdom to the participants.

Open communication is important. Children should know that they can come to you with any problem and you won't flip out on them. Be involved in your children's lives. But this doesn't mean that you should be hovering over them all of the time. In that smothering scenario, children may never develop the self-discipline needed to make their own moral decisions. If the parent is always there, the child won't grow. But involved a parent must be.

Explain to them the effects of drugs on the body. Explain the legal consequences of drug use. A conviction for a drug offense can lead to time in prison and cost you your job, your driver's license, a scholarship, or a college loan. Make it clear that you don't want your kids to use drugs and that you will be disappointed if they do. Explain how drug use hurts other people, not just the one doing the drugs. If your child has tried drugs, be honest about your disappointment, but emphasize that you still love him or her.

If your child has access to painkillers, keep a watchful eye. At Gateway Rehabilitation Center, Patrick wrote, "I got my wisdom teeth pulled that year and was prescribed Vicodin…I finished the bottle in a matter of days." And if a family member takes prescription drugs, keep them locked up. Over 90 percent of heroin users started with prescription pills. The pill habit can cost $150 per day. But the heroin habit may only cost about $40 per day. Out of financial necessity, the pill user often moves on to heroin.

While children's lives shouldn't be so regimented that they have no opportunity to make their own decisions, their lives shouldn't be so free and open that they can come and go without the parents' knowledge and consent. Research shows that when parents set harsh rules or no rules, kids are more likely to try drugs. The harsh rules stifle the child, and once the opportunity for freedom presents itself, a free-for-all ensues. And having no rules is like driving across a mile-high bridge with no guard rails. One can cross a particular bridge a thousand times and never use those guard rails. But it is comforting to know that they are there. Make clear rules and enforce them consistently.

Stay close to your children. Cultivate an atmosphere of love. Children will rebel; there will be heated words exchanged. But don't despair. In everything, put on love. If your child hollers, "I hate you," simply return a kind-sounding, "I'll always love you." If your unmarried daughter announces that she is pregnant, simply embrace her and assure her that everything will be OK. If a child admits that he or she did something wrong, first off, thank the child for his or her honesty.

Be a positive example for your child. This is evident in Patrick's drug biography that he penned at Gateway. He wrote, "Ever since I was young, I remember wondering what drugs felt like. I wondered, What does that beer do to my uncles and aunts at family events? What do cigarettes taste like? Why do people do it, and why do they seem so silly and happy?" Are your children seeing parents who are addicted to their own substances? The saying goes, little pitchers have big ears. The kids are always watching and listening. They can spot hypocrisy and insincerity. It does little good to tell your child to avoid drugs if the parent is always holding a glass of wine or smokes like a chimney. Remember that you set the example. Avoid contradictions between your words and your actions. Any alcohol consumption should be in moderation. Don't smoke cigarettes in front of the kids, and never use drugs. Patrick's biography also stated, "All of us smoked cigarettes too at that time. So we just thought we were the cat's @#$ for our adult-like behaviors we partook in. I guess that was how adults enjoyed themselves."

Though Anne and I do not drink alcohol on a regular basis or smoke cigarettes, somehow Patrick got the idea that drinking and smoking are the adult thing to do. I admit that a couple of times a year, I might have tied one on. But I did my best to conceal it from my children. On the other hand, numerous participants at family events took shot after shot of alcohol, and it became a major event to gather in a circle to drink. And the fun times he saw increased his desire to experience the same.

I absolutely do not blame any of them for the choices Patrick made in his life. God gave him a free will. He bears full responsibility for his actions. But I do think that many people are oblivious to the possible ill effects of the impression they make on others. The participants in these drinking circles didn't necessarily have a drinking problem. The annual event may have been the only time of the year that they drank. However, when somebody who has a weakness in this area decides to emulate them, problems ensue. When Patrick is home, I do not drink alcohol at all as a sign of solidarity with him. We were close with Patrick's cousin Ronnie. When he celebrated one year of being clean, we had a party for him, with nonalcoholic sparkling wine.

Pay attention to your child's friends. Based on statistics, drugs are introduced in middle school and high school to 30 percent of teenagers. From this, about 22 percent of them have friends who use illegal drugs. In Patrick's Gateway biography, he stated:

> As time went on, I turned many of my friends on to it, and soon enough, we were smoking pot on the regular and drinking my friend's mom's boxed wine. My other friend Bob would have us over often and we would have our way with his dad's Crown Royal! As I experimented more, I lost a lot of my friends, because I was more extreme, I guess. They made the right move though. I hung out with the potheads. By tenth grade, all my friends were the people I got high with. We were just skating through life in one big haze of smoke.

Be wary when your child suddenly begins to hang around with a different crowd.

As a parent, be at ease with your children. Get to know what makes them tick. Don't expect to be perfect, but approach everything with perfect confidence that, together with God's help, you will do your best. Remember, spouses, the best thing that you can do for your kids is to love their father or mother. Though everything is done in love, keep your ears and eyes open. It is written in scripture, "Behold, I am sending you out as sheep in the midst of wolves, so be wise as serpents and innocent as doves" (Matt. 10:16). There are evil forces and powers that want you and want your child. This is a battle. It is a spiritual battle. Spiritual battles are waged with spiritual tools. And one of the greatest spiritual tools is humility. Thus, though we are going into battle as wise serpents, we claim innocence, purity, humility, and dovelike gentleness as our greatest assets.

Alcoholics Anonymous has a twelve-step program that can lead to recovery. The following is an abbreviated version:

1. I admit that I am powerless over alcohol—that my life has become unmanageable.
2. I come to believe that a power greater than myself can restore me to sanity.
3. I make a decision to turn my will and my life over to the care of God (as I understand Him).
4. I make a searching and fearless moral inventory of myself.
5. I admit to God, to myself, and to another human being the exact nature of my wrongs.
6. I am entirely ready to have God remove all these defects of character.
7. I humbly ask Him to remove my shortcomings.

8. I will make a list of all persons I have harmed and am willing to make amends to them.
9. I make amends to such people wherever possible (except when this would injure them or others).
10. I continue to take personal inventory, and when I am wrong, I promptly admit it.
11. I seek through prayer and meditation to improve my conscious contact with God (as I understand Him), praying for knowledge of His will for me and the power to carry it out.
12. I will have a spiritual awakening as the result of these steps. I will try to carry this message to alcoholics (and drug abusers) and to practice these principles in all my affairs.

Following this program involves a thorough introspection. It also requires the support of another. The addict has changed as a result of his or her drug use. Substance abuse affects the frontal cortex of the brain, responsible for high-level decision making. And the limbic system is compromised. This is the emotion and reward center of the brain. Once the pleasure of the high is sensed here, the brain demands more. Additionally, drug abuse affects the brain's neurotransmitters, reducing its ability to produce dopamine and serotonin. Thus, being without the drug can cause depression. Drug abuse also tends to freeze emotional development. Remember that the person with whom you are dealing has many malfunctioning body systems. Be patient, and be strong.

Keep in mind that even though your loved one is going through a crisis, you are still allowed to be happy. Don't let shame take hold of you. Bring the drug problem out of the shadows and into the light of day. Seek help and support for yourself.

Once a choice is made to give up drug use, the battle is only half won. It is crucial to not relax. Remember the parable of the return of an unclean spirit.

> Now when the unclean spirit goes out of a man, it passes through waterless places seeking rest, and does not find it. Then it says, "I will return to my house from which I came"; and when it comes, it finds it unoccupied, swept, and put in order. Then it goes and takes along with it seven other spirits more wicked than itself, and they go in and live there; and the last state of that man becomes worse than the first. That is the way it will also be with this evil generation.
> (Matt. 12:43–45)

A person who is newly converted or one who attempts to make things right will often meet great obstacles in recovery. Once the devil has hold of a person, he does not want to let go. As he sees this person slipping away from evil, he will do everything in his power to get the person back. Help with recovery is vital, but prolonged follow-up is essential as well. Just as former users must never let down their guard, the spiritual forces that prompted the recovery must be an ongoing process.

It is helpful to know that drug addiction is not always a moral failing. The initial decision to use illegal drugs is indeed a failure of adherence to righteous moral action. But once addicted, the will to resist is overwhelmed by the drug's power over the body. And for those with an inherited addictive predisposition, the drugs add fuel to the fire.

Avail yourself to the power of prayer. Ask for the prayers of others. Attend church. For ten years, with nearly every spiritual person I met, I asked them to pray for Patrick. And their prayers have been answered. Luke 11:18 tells of a man who needed bread for his guests late at night. He knocked at his neighbor's door, but the man tried to send him away. However, the needy man kept knocking and knocking. Finally the man relented and gave all that was needed. The parable concludes, "I tell you, even though he will not get up and give him anything because he is his friend, yet because of his persistence he will get up and give him as much as he needs" (Luke 11:8). God doesn't need our prayers, but He wants our prayers. It was only when I accepted my helplessness before God and turned everything over to Jesus through Mary that my family and Patrick received the Heavenly intervention needed in getting him to Cenacolo. Pray fervently and pray often.

Above all, put on love. First of all, love God. Offering more love to God enables one to give more love to others. Having a relationship with God gives divine strength and fortitude. Your personal motto could be, "Lord, there is nothing that can happen today that You and I can't handle together."

Love is stronger than hate. Love is stronger than evil. Love is stronger than addiction. Love never fails. In the Bible we read, "Three things will last forever—faith, hope, and love—and the greatest of these is love" (1 Cor. 13:13).

Amen.

Helpful Resources
There is not just one path to recovery. Each individual has a path that is as unique as his or her own personality. What works for one may not work for another. Listed below are a few of the many drug-rehabilitation and support programs available. Discuss the choices with the addicted person. Pray over the matter. Make a choice that best suits the needs of the addict. But make a choice. Do not delay. Not making a choice is choosing to do nothing. Do something, and do not delay.

Choosing a Drug Treatment Program
http://www.helpguide.org/articles/addiction/choosing-a-drug-treatment-program.htm
Call 1-800-662-HELP (4357) What to Look for in Substance Abuse Rehab.

Al-Anon/Alateen Family Groups
http://www.al-anon.org/ or (613) 723-8484
Offering strength and hope for friends and family of drug and alcohol abusers.

National Suicide Prevention Lifeline
www.suicidepreventionlifeline.org or 1 (800) 273-TALK (8255)
They want to help you find a reason to keep living.

Cenacolo
http://www.comunitacenacolo.org/ (See website for regional contact numbers.)
Cenacolo proposes a simple, disciplined, family style of life, based on the rediscovery of the essential gifts of prayer and work, true friendship, sacrifice, and faith in Jesus.

SpiritLife
http://www.spiritliferecovery.org or 724-465-2165
This program will treat the whole person and family: medically, psychologically, spiritually, and emotionally. (Based in western Pennsylvania.)

Teen Challenge (not just for teens)
https://www.teenchallenge.cc/plaintext/home/home.aspx or 417-581-2181

Teen Challenge believes in second chances. Their purpose is to facilitate life transformation of those whose lives have been affected by drug use and/or abuse.

Gateway
http://www.gatewayrehab.org/ or 800-472-1177
Gateway Rehabilitation Center is a positive force in the prevention, treatment, education, and research of substance abuse and alcoholism.

Greenbriar
http://www.greenbriar.net/ or 1-800-637-HOPE (4673)
Their mission, since 1985, has been to provide quality chemical-dependency and dual treatment to the clients they serve. (Pittsburgh area)

Narcotics Anonymous
https://www.na.org/
Their vision is that every addict in the world has the chance to experience their message and find the opportunity for a new way of life.

Alcoholics Anonymous
http://www.aa.org/
Alcoholics Anonymous is an international fellowship of men and women who have had a drinking problem. It is nonprofessional, self-supporting, multiracial, apolitical, and available almost everywhere.

Substance Abuse Information Center
http://www.addictioncareoptions.com/ or 800-784-6776
Offering information about every aspect of substance-abuse disorders and recommends the best rehabilitation facilities available.

Treatment Referral Service
http://www.samhsa.gov/find-help/national-helpline or 1-800-662-HELP (4357)
For individuals and family members facing mental-health and/or substance-use disorders. This service provides referrals to local treatment facilities and support groups.

Drug Rehab Choices
http://www.rehabs.com/ or 1-888-992-3387
Offering sixty- and ninety-day programs.

Free Inpatient Drug Rehab
http://www.inpatientdrugrehabcenters.com/inpatient-drug-rehab-programs/free-inpatient-drug-rehab/ or 1-800-895-1695
Referrals to free treatment centers.

Salvation Army Harbor Light Center
http://salvationarmyusa.org/usn/harbor-lights
They seek to bring hope to those who have fallen captive to substance abuse.

Epilogue

One may wonder about the people who hung out with Patrick and used drugs with him. Some have recovered, while others have not. While doing prison ministry in my town, I meet quite a few inmates who know my son. When they learn of his transformation from user to missionary, it is typical for their jaws to drop open. One of those fellows who was a friend with Patrick told me that twelve of his friends have overdosed and died. More were killed in car accidents that resulted from driving while under the influence of illegal drugs. Here is a rundown of the destinies of those mentioned in this story.

Mac
His recovery came hard. He didn't find the road to recovery until he had hit rock bottom. Mac was arrested on drug charges. His parents refused to bail him out of jail. At the time, he was very resentful of them and vented his anger toward them. But this turn of events proved to be Mac's pivotal experience. Upon being released, he set himself to get clean. This he did.

Mac went to school and is now working in the medical profession. Due to his criminal record, his acceptance into the medical field was quite tenuous. But he had solidly turned himself around and was eventually allowed to obtain the license necessary for his employment. Mac is married and has a child. He and his wife are practicing Catholics.

Ronnie
He traveled a long road to recovery. Ronnie had dropped out of high school. He drifted from job to job. Eventually he was arrested for burglary. His time in jail did him good. Upon release, Ronnie got his GED and found gainful employment.

Ronnie began his illegal drug use for various reasons. He was bored. He had nothing to do. He felt peer pressure and wanted to fit in with the crowd.

Once he used drugs, things seemed great. There was fun, acceptance, exhilaration, camaraderie, and pleasure. Life was a blast. But these positive feelings eventually began slipping away. The fun gave way to pain. The acceptance gave way to isolation. Exhilaration gave way to despondency. Camaraderie gave way to shame. And his pleasure gave way to paranoia.

Seeing his deteriorating situation, Ronnie wanted out. But he didn't know how to escape his addiction. He tried many times to stop, telling himself that this was the end of his drug use. But that resolve never held. He didn't know how to stop using.

It wasn't until he ended up in jail that things began to change. Due to his incarceration, he was finally clean. Once released, Ronnie promised himself that he wouldn't use illegal drugs again. But it was still OK for him to drink alcohol. After all, it was legal. There was no connection between drugs and alcohol, or so he thought.

Within a couple of weeks, he got into a fight and was arrested. Adding insult to injury, he was also charged with parole violation because he was drunk. So back to jail he went. For thirty days more he stewed in the slammer.

Once released, Ronnie was court-ordered to attend Gateway Rehabilitation Center. For forty-five days, he went through the vigorous and thorough training. It seems that he mostly got the message, for upon completion, he was again resolved to stay away from drugs.

There was a lot on his mind. He considered the possibility that he might be sent to state prison. He prayed—a lot. And he asked, "Why me, God? Why am I living this terrible life?" For four months he worked the program. But soon rationalizations popped up. He put himself into an environment of close proximity to drugs.

One night Ronnie found himself at a party. Someone thrust a bottle of vodka into his hand. This was his moment of decision. The tension was replete. With his two hands grasping the bottle, he felt as if he might shatter it in his palms. Sweat poured from his forehead. The adage he had learned at AA came to mind. "One drink is too many, and one thousand is never enough." He knew this in his mind, but it seemed as if there was no way out for him.

Wanting out, Ronnie ran to his car. As he drove away, he still had the bottle. It was secured between his legs. In desperation he began praying again. He decided to test God. He prayed, "If this is not what I should be doing, show me. God, give me a sign!" With that, he put the bottle to his lips and took a big gulp. Immediately, the car let out a clunking noise and broke down. Now stranded, he began walking along the road while finishing off the bottle of vodka. He was in an awful mess. To make matters worse, he also got beat up that night.

Arriving home in the wee hours of the morning, he dropped into bed. His mind was swirling in conflict. He'd been to jail. He'd lost his job. He'd fallen off the wagon. And now his car was broken down. What else bad could happen? He wanted to be done with his addictions but didn't know how. His mind screamed, "God, show me the way out!"

On that afternoon his mom tried to get him out of bed. Ronnie clung to his covers and wouldn't move. He was too ashamed of himself to uncover. The blanket gave him a cloak of invisibility. He didn't want to reveal to his mom the person he'd become. His self-respect was gone. Then he began berating his mother and blaming her for all of his problems. Everything was her fault. Why didn't she do this and do that? Why was she always bothering him? If it wasn't for her, he would…on and on it went.

Finally she had had enough. For years she had done everything possible to help him. Every kind gesture of hers was met with ingratitude. Every bit of help she had given to him was not acknowledged or was met with a grunt at best. She had been put through the wringer with his drug abuse, arrests, and hurtful and disrespectful behavior. This was it! Ronnie's mother told him to leave the house and to not come back.

But he wouldn't leave. Arguments ensued. The tension was horrific. Ronnie was in a full-blown rage. But even in the difficult act of self-preservation of kicking him out of the house, Ronnie's mother offered kindness. She had arranged for her brother (me) to come and get Ronnie. As the dispute continued, Ronnie decided that he was going to run. He didn't know where he was going, but he was going somewhere—and fast. He stormed to his room to pack some clothes.

Emerging into the living room with a garbage bag full of his possessions, he was intent on storming out—to where, he didn't know. Then he spied his godfather, Uncle Paul. "What are you doing here?" Ronnie asked.

"You're coming with me," was my reply.

Ronnie returned to his room to pack the rest of his possessions. Ronnie wondered, "Could this be the beginning of a new life for me?" He then sheepishly went with his uncle Paul and lived with us for nearly a year.

To make a long story short, that prior evening was the last drink of alcohol, as well as his last use of illegal drugs. He needed a change of environment to help enact the changes he was attempting to make in his life. His parents had done their best to help him. But Ronnie had to do it himself. It took the trauma of being in prison, losing his job, losing his car, and losing his home to wake him up. The new home simply provided him with a new perspective and a fresh start. One year later our extended family celebrated Ronnie's 365 days clean. It was a joyful celebration!

Ronnie shared about his experience. He said that nobody can make you clean. Though others may help, you have to do it yourself, for yourself. Everybody has a bottom. But on drugs, there is always a deeper bottom. Not everybody is the same, and their recovery will come about in a way unique to them. For some it may take confrontation; for others a more passive approach may be needed. For some, a crisis is the turning point. Whatever your role in a loved one's recovery, remember this. Do something. Don't be a bystander.

It takes at least a year for the reward pathways in the brain to become rewired in the correct way. And it takes another year for recovery to gain traction. In the very best of circumstances, a bare minimum of three years of active recovery efforts is needed.

Whatever the method attempted, recovery is not guaranteed. But continuing to use drugs does have a guarantee. It guarantees a future that is hollow and a life that is empty. It guarantees suffering and pain. This pain is experienced not only by the user but by all those with whom the addict has close ties.

Ronnie attests that it was God who pulled him out of his slavery to drugs. And it is his faith in God that sustains him in his recovered life.

It was not until about three years clean that he considered himself as having a good chance to remain that way. But he is always on guard. An ex-user must always consider the possibility of falling back into the former addicted life. To this day, Ronnie remains vigilant and still attends NA meetings on at least a weekly basis.

Ronnie is married and has a child. He and his wife are also practicing Catholics. Ronnie has put his extensive knowledge of the drug culture to good use. He is a counselor for a drug-addiction-treatment center. Ronnie was a consultant in the writing of this story. As young boys, Patrick and Ronnie spoke of their future—that they might live beside each other, and so on. They also promised that they would choose each other as a godparent for one of their children. In 2014, Patrick became the godfather of Ronnie's baby girl.

Rachael
Though she didn't use illegal drugs, she was affected by them through her engagement to Patrick. Rachael has moved on. She is married and has two children. Rachael does not regret her relationship with Patrick. He helped her get through a tough time in her life.

Nate
He is currently in jail. Nate had moved to California and attempted to join the drug scene there. But the law caught up with him. He's been in and out of jail in several states. Nate has certainly fallen short of his potential. With his intelligence and the status of his parents, he could have done nearly anything he desired.

Chrissy (Patrick's girlfriend)
She has attempted several times to give up drugs. Though her brother died of a drug overdose, this was not enough to motivate her to break the habit. She has had a responsible job in the family business and has a good head on her shoulders. But currently she is in jail with an eighteen-month sentence. I feel she will eventually overcome these detriments and clean herself up.

Bill
Bill overdosed on heroin and died.

Dave
Dave overdosed on medical patches and died.

Bob
He didn't delve very far into illegal drugs. But it seems that today, as a businessman, his drug of choice is alcohol. He has had a couple of DUI arrests.

Cathie
Cathie traveled a long, hard road to recovery. She became so dragged down and burned out that she had no choice but to get clean or die. She is now a mother. Patrick is the godfather of her baby.

Dirk
He had one of those crisis conversions. With the death of his mother, which was most likely the result of her drug use, Dirk was crushed. He decided that the drugs that took his mother would not take him. He is living a life that is mostly clean, and he is doing OK.

Betty
She never gave up the drug habit. Betty is deceased. She died while in her forties, most likely from the complications of drug abuse.

Dr. Mirro
He was arrested as a result of a sting operation. Dr. Mirro is in federal prison for dispensing drugs illegally to his patients. Some years earlier, I had actually reported Dr. Mirro to the FBI. I'd seen numerous bottles of pain killer, bearing his name, prescribed to drug addicts. The FBI later contacted me and asked me to participate in a sting operation against Dr. Mirro, but I refused. Apparently, they found another person to do that job.

Sherry
She attended a prestigious college and pursued her dream of becoming a pig farmer.

Others
I've met many of Patrick's friends while doing prison ministry. Josh, Egan, Adam, Dave, Brian, Chris, Ed, and others are each surprised to learn that I am Patrick's father. They are amazed when I tell them of Patrick's missionary work. "Pat is a missionary? You've got to be kidding." And they always want to hear more. One young man told me that he has heard dozens of recovery stories through AA and NA. He remarked that Patrick's story is the most amazing he has ever heard.

Patrick
Patrick stayed in the Cenacolo Community as a way of giving back. For the first eighteen months after completing his three years of recovery, he became the head of a newly opened Cenacolo Community in Alabama. Once the Community was established, he became a missionary in an orphan mission in Argentina.

This missionary work is an arduous challenge. Taking care of these kids is a sublime task, yet at times it can be degrading. It is rewarding yet taxing as well. It is simple yet complex. It is fulfilling and also draining. Caring for them is invigorating, and it is exhausting. It is inspiring, and it can also be discouraging. It is holy, and it is the will of God. Caring for these young ones is fulfilling every one of the corporal and spiritual works of mercy. And God's bountiful hand is upon them.

The Corporal works of mercy:	How he fulfills this:
• Feed the hungry	Done three times per day
• Give drink to the thirsty	Many times per day

- Clothe the naked — Clothed, washed, dried
- Shelter the homeless — Yes indeed
- Visit the sick — Every time
- Ransom the captive — From the streets
- Bury the dead — When the time comes

<u>The Spiritual works of mercy</u>:   <u>How he fulfills this</u>:
- Instruct the ignorant — Every day
- Counsel the doubtful — Quite often
- Admonish sinners — When necessary
- Bear wrongs patiently — Lots of that going on
- Forgive offences willingly — Every time
- Comfort the afflicted — Every moment
- Pray for living and dead — With every thought

Living among the orphans enables people to give away all of their love. It's awesome! Usually it is returned, but at times it is not. Ministering to these children demands a big heart and a strong body. The kids have a large hole needing to be filled, and they look to the former addicts of Cenacolo to fill that hole.

These kids, many of whom were street kids, are also brought into the light through Cenacolo. These tough, street-wise boys under Patrick's care are made to be responsible. They arise at 5:30 a.m., make their beds, and then go to the chapel for prayer. Here they kneel on the stone floor. Then they walk a very steep five-mile climb to school. Upon returning home, they resume their cleaning duties and then go back to the chapel for an evening rosary. And they also have time to play.

The tasks of the adults are never ending. But all his work is done with joy! Patrick's giving makes him incredibly happy.

A couple of years ago, I visited the mission. I participated with Patrick in the day-to-day activities. After getting the kids to bed one night, Patrick and I had a heart-to-heart about giving love without expecting it to be returned. In the past, Patrick had wondered if he gave love to the boys only because he knew he would get love in return.

About this time, a person named Rodreigo arrived in Community. He was severely autistic. Patrick was put in charge of him. Rodreigo needed to be cleaned and dressed every day. He needed constant tending. And yet, Rodreigo had no awareness of the effort and sacrifice needed to take care of him. And Rodreigo was incapable of returning any of the love given to him. Patrick now knew that he could indeed give love with no expectation of return.

Rodreigo is a study in contrast. It is obvious that not having him in Community would greatly reduce the workload on the adults. Just taking care of the children is more than enough work for anybody. When Roderigo first came to Community, he came from an experience where he had been tied to a chair for several years. Let free at Cenacolo, he had a massive convulsion, attacking people and being totally out of control. It seemed as if they would have to turn him away. But Mother Elvira, who was present at the time, insisted that he stay. In her wisdom, she knew that the efforts expended by taking care of him would produce abundant grace for the Cenacolo Community. Though it is difficult to care for him, God has repaid Cenacolo many times over for their compassion and care of Roderigo. Patrick was given sole responsibility for Roderigo, taking care of his every need.

So it is with the spiritual world. What seems to be a detriment can indeed provide the path to our salvation. Though Roderigo is very difficult to care for, the love and trust in God that is exhibited through this care provides a conduit to God's abundant love and blessings.

A specialist in Italy took on Rodrigo's case and tested him. The doctor set out a bag of candy on his desk to assess Rodrigo's reaction. Roderigo picked up the bag and shared it with those in the room before taking any for himself. The doctor was astounded that Roderigo had thought of others before himself. The doctor said that due to Roderigo's condition, it should be impossible that he would act in such a way. But it did happen. Roderigo's experience of sharing in community had conditioned him to this action. Nurture verses nature? It seems that nurture is prevailing.

What about your addict? Can nurture change his or her nature that led to drug abuse? The answer is a resounding *yes*. Loving and prayerful nurturing can make a difference.

Through this giving of himself, Patrick has become transformed.

He is not only a new man; he is a renewed man.

Patrick is a polar opposite of what he was when abusing drugs. His entire demeanor indicates clearly his interior happiness. The selfless giving of his life to God has profoundly changed him. People have mentioned that he has a holy aura about him. I could thank God every moment of my life, for the rest of my life, and it wouldn't be enough to thank Him for saving Patrick. My son, who was dead, is now alive. Praise God from Whom all blessings flow!

Less than a year ago, Patrick told his mother and me that he had written a letter to the head priest of Cenacolo about some feelings he had been having. Patrick inquired as to his future with Cenacolo. Fr. Stefano wrote back to him with instructions for the Community. Patrick was called to live at a Cenacolo Community in Loreto, Italy.

Patrick went to live among the Cenacolo religious there. The reason for this change was for Patrick to enter into a special period of discernment.

Patrick spent about six months in Italy discerning if God was calling him to become a Catholic priest. Concluding this discernment, Patrick felt that he was not being called to become a priest. His heart was still with the Argentinian orphans, but his slot there had been filled by another. So he came home for a break and for more time to decide his future. Fr. Stefano told him, "Go home and see what happens."

While home, he was asked to volunteer to help in the preparations for the opening of a drug-detox center near his hometown. The development and opening of this center, in the works for several years, had been the ardent desire of several local priests who are familiar with the Cenacolo "school of life." The first stage of this endeavor was to open the detox center. The second stage is to create a Cenacolo-like residential complex. Using the Cenacolo model, though unaffiliated with Cenacolo, the priests' hope was that Mother Elvira's vision can be implemented there.

After meeting with the director of the new Living in the Spirit Center, Patrick was asked to become part of the paid staff. Having been given free housing, he resides at the complex and offers direction and inspiration to the staff. Additionally, Patrick offers counseling to those entering the facility. There is also plenty of physical labor involved in remodeling the older buildings and grounds. Just as at Cenacolo, work, prayer, and ministry fill his life.

Patrick is currently engaged to be married.

And I have more good news to share. Upon Patrick's return to the United States, he has undergone medical treatment for his hepatitis.

New drugs are available that will cure the disease. Patrick is currently clean of this virus. Praise God!

Witnessing these events, I marvel at God's goodness, and I am awed by His Divine Providence. Even in our weakness, God weaves the events of our lives to bring about His will. He has taken a beat-down, out-of-control addict who was close to death and made of him a vibrant, faith-filled young man, full of life and love. God's blessings have indeed been overwhelmingly wonderful upon us!

And should his vocation change, all is well. For whatever we do, as long as it is God's plan for our life, is good. Not all are called to be priests, missionaries, or counselors. But all are called. God has a unique mission for each of us. Finding that mission and living that mission will surely bring us success in life. In Christ, all is good!

Is there hope for the addict in your life? Most certainly! All things are possible with God.

Change can be achieved. Transformation is possible. Christ is calling the addict and is indeed calling each one of us. He is calling us from the darkness we've created into the light of His presence. Perhaps He is calling on you especially. You may be the one whose prayers provide the tipping point for a loved one's recovery.

Keep in mind that recovery does not usually come all at once. Patrick's recovery traveled a hilly road of numerous ups and downs. At times healing seemed to be complete, only to be dashed by the circumstances of life. He experienced at least four recoveries followed by four relapses. But the addict must keep moving forward. Complete healing does exist. And as you move forward, keep your eyes on the prize. That prize is great indeed.

Thank you, Patrick, for showing us that recovery is possible.

Thank You Lord, for offering us the grace necessary for our state in life. May each of us avail ourselves to Your abundant mercy and Your loving call. With our every breath, may we be in service to You. With every beat of our heart, may it be with love for You. Let our every thought, word and deed be in accordance with your holy Will. Let Your grace be showered down upon us and upon our families. Please give us abundant faith, hope and love for our journey in life. Praised be Your most Holy Name, now and forevermore. Amen.

My ardent prayer is that you and your loved ones will soon be Returning to the Light.

Patrick's Words

When I reflect on the past thirty-one years since my birth, I become more and more convinced that there is no such thing as a coincidence. "Chance" or other words, such as "luck," "fortune," or "karma," can all be explained as glimpses of God's hand in our lives. God's actions and His Divine Providence are all around us. But often we do not recognize these interventions.

Since I was young, I had been brought up in the Catholic faith. I always knew the difference between right and wrong. But in my adolescence, I was blinded by an evil power that seemed to be greater than me and greater than my power to resist. But despite my bad decisions and my sinful behavior, I remained in God's hands and in His love. Though my experience was lived out by offending God, I was never far away from His saving power. This was true despite my best efforts to run away. I believe that no one is ever far from God's saving power. But we are given free will and have the power to accept or reject God's mercy. Our Creator leaves it up to us to choose. We are all free. We are free to choose doing good, and we are free to choose doing bad. We are free to choose love and are free to choose hate. We are free to choose God, and we are free to choose evil. We are free to choose life, and we are free to choose death.

Personally, when I ultimately chose to take the first definitive steps toward my Lord, my former life of sin and depravity ceased to exist. I embraced a new reality. It is a reality of God's overwhelming love for me. This awareness of God's indwelling love is what caused the needed change in me. He was always there with His love, but it was necessary that I accept that love.

Before my return, I had lived my life wrapped up in the past and worrying about the future. I was full of regret of what I had done and was full of apprehension of what tomorrow might bring. Eventually, though, I came to realize that all I had was the present. Yesterday is gone and tomorrow may never come. God reigns in the present. He has given me this very moment that I am now living. I cannot change the past, and the future is unknowable. So living in the present seems to be the most logical way to live. Now, what will I choose to do with this present moment before me? That is the question. Our reality is always in the present. What I do right now is what matters. The journey begins with one step. I must make every step toward God.

And so I say carpe diem. Seize the day. I don't want to miss any chance that God gives me to serve Him. God has taken me from my hometown to Italy, and from Italy to the missions in Argentina, and back again to Italy. I could not have planned out this fruitful life for myself. All I have to do is try to follow His Will in every moment and trust! Trust is the key.

Today I trust in God. God wants good things for me, and I want to allow Him to work through me. So I choose to serve. I thank God for everything that I have lived up to this very moment. The good and the bad—it was all useful. It has brought me to exactly where I am right now, in His all-merciful and all-powerful hands. He has embraced me with His eternal light.

Conclusion

The unedited completion of this book occurred on September 8, 2015. Providentially, this date is also the traditional date given to the birthday of the Blessed Mother, the Mother of Jesus. It was her intercession years ago, and my giving of Patrick to her care, that proved to be the turning point for Patrick's eventual recovery. It was Mary, the Mother of Jesus, who guided Patrick's heart. Mary guided Patrick's heart to the Heart of Jesus. At the wedding feast of Cana, Mary gave instructions to the waiters concerning the lack of wine for the wedding feast. Mary told them, "Do whatever He (Jesus) tells you." Patrick was given those very same instructions.

And it was the Eucharistic Lord, present in the golden monstrance that captured Patrick's heart, strengthened his faith, and transformed his life. Mary indeed, led Patrick to Jesus. Then the love and mercy of God penetrated Patrick's being, and broke the chains of addiction that held Patrick captive for so many years. Patrick was infused with knowledge of the truth of God's love for him. "Then you will know the truth, and the truth will set you free." (John 8:32) Patrick has been set free.

And since Patrick accepted the words of Jesus, his life has never been the same. The religion that he once critiqued is the religion that guided him back to a state of grace. His life has never been better. Patrick's life has never been so fruitful. His new reality is far beyond what he had ever imagined for himself. This life, lived in Christ, is one of continual Faith, Hope, and Love. And this love of Christ and His movement in our lives is a true foretaste of the bliss that awaits us in Heaven.

Concerning addiction, remember that the solution to this addiction is Jesus Christ. Jesus is beckoning us always, from the darkness into the light of His presence. Amen.

Made in the USA
San Bernardino, CA
25 April 2017